Bordertown Café

Bordertown Café

Kelly Rebar

TALONBOOKS

2003

Copyright © 2003 Kelly Rebar

Talonbooks
P.O. Box 2076, Vancouver, British Columbia, Canada V6B 3S3
www.talonbooks.com

Typeset in New Baskerville and printed and bound in Canada.

Second Printing: August 2007

The publisher gratefully acknowledges the financial support of the Canada Council for the Arts; the Government of Canada through the Book Publishing Industry Development Program; and the Province of British Columbia through the British Columbia Arts Council for our publishing activities.

Bordertown Café was originally published by Blizzard Publishing in 1987.

National Library of Canada Cataloguing in Publication Data

Rebar, Kelly, 1956–
  Bordertown cafe / Kelly Rebar.

  A play.
  ISBN 0-88922-477-3

  I. Title.
PS8585.E337B6 2003   C812'.54   C2003-910137-1
PR9199.3.R415B6 2003

ISBN-10: 0-88922-477-3
ISBN-13: 978-0-88922-477-3

For my good friend Anne McGrath

Bordertown Café premiered at the Blyth Festival in Blyth, Ontario on June 23, 1987 with the following cast:

JIMMY..Kevin Bundy
MARLENE..Laurel Paetz
MAXINE ....Lorna Wilson
JIM...Jerry Franken

Directed by Katherine Kaszas
Set and Costume Design by Allan Stitchbury
Lighting Design by Kevin Fraser

CHARACTERS

JIMMY, 17
MARLENE, 34, Jimmy's mother
MAXINE, 57, Marlene's mother
JIM, 62, Marlene's father

SCENE

A café on the Canadian side of the Alberta/ Montana border. The present [late 1980s.]

SET

The kitchen of the café. It is a kitchen which bridges public and private use. In addition to the trays of dishes and cups, ketchup bottles and relish jars, the lard can, the grill and work area, there are indications that this kitchen is a family centre. There is a small kitchen table with chairs, magazines, bills, a paperback or two. The café is old but very clean, organized in its own way. There is an order window and a swinging door to the front of the café. There is a screen door leading outside. There is a door or passageway to the back suite. Jimmy's bedroom either introduces the back suite and one must pass through his room to get to the back, or it is in some way shown to be a room without privacy. The single bed takes up most of the space. Typical teenage boy things are about and, again, there is a tidiness. The closed, tight space of the café is contrasted by a sense of overwhelming prairie sky that surrounds the set.

ACT ONE

The sound of a combine approaching. The sun begins to rise. JIMMY is asleep in his bed. Light enters the kitchen and lends a photographic quality to the place, as if things have been caught in time. The sound of the combine reaches a point, then begins to fade away. As the sound fades, the sunrise approaches its peak. Just as the light seems to hold still, the sound of the combine ceases. JIMMY snaps awake. He gets out of bed and goes into the kitchen to look out through the screen door. The sun carries on, the kitchen loses its quality, and things appear functional. JIMMY goes back to his room, and goes back to bed. The sound of a meadowlark is heard. The phone rings. It rings again.

JIMMY:
> Am I getting that Mum?

> *MARLENE enters from the back suite, doing up her robe. She crosses to the phone in the kitchen.*

MARLENE:
> (*answering*) We're awake, Mum. (*realizing her error*) Oh, hi. You comin' up? Yeah, 'cept for he's got school startin' today, eh.

JIMMY:
> (*immediately*) No, I don't, Friday's just registration.

MARLENE:

> What about?

JIMMY:

> What about what about?

MARLENE:

> Oh.

> > *Pause.*

JIMMY:

> Oh what Mum?

MARLENE:

> If that's what he wants.

JIMMY:

> If he's pickin' me up for a haul, I can't go with him,
> Grandad and me got a crop to get off.

MARLENE:

> Just sec. (*to JIMMY*) Am I tryna talk?

JIMMY:

> There's certain considerations.

MARLENE:

> (*back to the phone*) Up to him.

JIMMY:

> (*throwing the covers back*) Wait—wait—

MARLENE:

> 'Kay then bye.

> > *JIMMY freezes, then falls back to bed. MARLENE hangs
> > up, keeping her hand on the receiver a spell. She crosses
> > to the little kitchen table and lights a cigarette. A tanker
> > can be heard gearing by and fading away. MARLENE
> > waits for it to go. The light makes another transition.*

MARLENE:

> Get up, Jimmy.

JIMMY:

Where's he at?

MARLENE crosses to the door to look out. Pause.

JIMMY:

Well, if he's just leaving Wyoming now he won't reach the border 'til way past—

MARLENE:

Bring me out my curling iron.

MARLENE goes back to the table to place her cigarette down in the ashtray.

JIMMY:

Is my dad just leaving Wyoming now, I says.

MARLENE:

I'm not beatin' around the bush. I'm gettin' right to the point. Your dad's—just leaving Wyoming now. (*MARLENE takes a quarter from the tip jar and looks toward Jimmy's room.*) And not only that he got married. (*She starts to exit to the front, stopping briefly.*) Make your bed.

She exits. JIMMY jumps out of bed and throws on his jeans. A song comes on the jukebox from out front. JIMMY goes to the kitchen to wait for MARLENE to re-enter.

JIMMY:

(*hollering to the front*) And here I didn't even know he was goin' with her! (*He realizes the give-away of his lie and hollers louder to cover it.*) He say who to?!

MARLENE comes back in, heading for the back suite.

MARLENE:

(*as if it is all one word*) No he never Linda Somebody.

MARLENE sets to making Jimmy's bed. JIMMY follows her into his room to take over from her, but MARLENE

finishes any job she starts and JIMMY is forced to watch,
guilt-ridden and idle.

JIMMY:

Well, it don't matter to me, does it matter to you? He
got married?

MARLENE:

(*disguised*) Does it look like it matters to me? (*continues*
with the bed)

JIMMY:

(*watching*) Well, that's great.

MARLENE:

Colour hair she got?

> *JIMMY starts to answer but doesn't finish. He watches*
> *MARLENE fuss with the bed. He exits back to the suite*
> *and returns with a shaving kit and towel. He watches*
> *MARLENE fuss with the bedspread. Finally:*

JIMMY:

Quit makin' that bed!

MARLENE:

I knew it! Every time your dad comes up to Canada, I
end up gettin' yelled at! And I know I shoulda got you
a new bedspread four, five years ago, but I didn't!

JIMMY:

What!

MARLENE:

Didn't, Jimmy, didn't. Should change it to my name,
Marlene Didn't. Didn't wanna fix this place up 'cause
why would a person wanna sock a bunch of money
into a back suite when she's gonna buy the Mathison
place when it comes up for sale? Mathison place
comes up for sale, did I buy it—? No, I didn't. I don't
have the Mathison place and I don't have the fixed-up

back suite and now you're—and he's—and this is for a little boy, this bedspread, it's for a little boy.

> *Pause.*

JIMMY:
> Did Dad say what time he was gettin' here?

MARLENE:
> Four!

JIMMY:
> Four?

MARLENE:
> And you're standing there tellin' me she's got me beat all to heck, this gal.

JIMMY:
> I got conditioning at four.

MARLENE:
> I know that without ever layin' eyes on her.

JIMMY:
> No, Mum.

MARLENE:
> Eh?

JIMMY:
> Don't think that.

MARLENE:
> Well, this is it. How does he think he could do better'n me with the kinda girls he 'sociates with? Answer me that. Oh, those American girls, don't tell me about American girls, I lived down there, I know exactly what they're capable of down there.

JIMMY:
> This is mattering, Dad getting married.

MARLENE:

No it isn't mattering and I'll tell you why it is. (*pause*) See Jimmy, uh.

JIMMY:

What?

MARLENE:

I—I—I'm not sayin' it's any great shakes livin' here, but there's a lot o' kids out there without a pillow to call their own, they'd think your room there's a palace. (*She has exited back.*)

JIMMY:

I got no problems with it neither.

MARLENE:

(*off*) And you can stay out the farm any night the week you want.

> *She enters carrying her curling iron, which she takes to the outlet nearest the table.*

JIMMY:

I know—I—oh, I was gonna get that.

MARLENE:

Gonna, that's another one—Jimmy Gonna and Marlene Didn't, we should move to Nashville and break into an act—speakin' of which I'm not going through the day with Mum song and dancing about your dad to me, not today.

JIMMY:

I won't say nothing but—

MARLENE:

I'm countin' on it.

JIMMY:

I have a complication I'd like to air.

MARLENE:
Yeah, well, he said he'd be here at four.

JIMMY:
Coach isn't caring if you're in harvest or not, he said if you wanna play hockey this year you can't miss conditioning. So if he's not carin' about harvest he'll care even less about Dad showin' up—

MARLENE:
Just be on that school bus.

JIMMY:
But Mum.

MARLENE:
(*exiting back*) And get washed.

JIMMY:
I'm cut before I even make the team? (*pause*) Mum.

MARLENE:
(*off*) What?

JIMMY:
This is kind of inconvenient. I can't be takin' off on no haul, I got a crop to get off. I got conditioning. Dad shoulda bin informed. (*pause*) Mum.

MARLENE:
(*off*) What?

JIMMY:
He won't even be here on time, he never is—the guy don't operate on Mountain Standard. But that's okay, Jimmy can count the trucks passin', waitin' on him. (*He takes his kit and towel and starts to head to the front, but stops, wheels around, and addresses the back suite.*) I wanted to start my last year off like a normal human hockey player. The plan was set. The whole time I'm out in that field I'm thinking, Jimmy?—I know you wrecked your truck, I know it's not exactly smooth in

that café but you bin around Grandad all summer long—just take after him and eat your Puff' Wheat like there's nothing the matter. I figgered today, oh, I'd show up at school, say hi to the guys, register, give the girls a quick once-over to see if there's any changes, and then saunter down to the Doughnut Hole—yes, me, Jimmy—saunter, huck a few bottle caps at the garbage can. Uh huh. Well shall we scrap that plan, Mum?—Number one, I'm up at the crack of dawn filled to the gills with guilt already for not bein' out in that field.

MARLENE:

(*off*) You're gettin' washed up, eh.

JIMMY:

"Hey Jimmy," the guys'll say. "Comin' down to the Hole?" "Sorry guys, can't." Carve it into my tombstone. "Sorry guys, can't." (*pause*) Mum?

MARLENE:

(*off*) Sorry guys, can't.

JIMMY:

The Hawks' game, a prime example. Game's over, we won, whole team come truckin' in here for Cokes and burgers and who do they find sittin' in that till? Mr. Humiliation, still waitin' on his off-and-on dad to turn up, take him on a haul. Not only could I a' played, I coulda come back and gone to sleep for five hours before his rig pulled up. Oh, but hockey games, they don't matter, sleep? Who needs it?—Hop on up, kid. If I wanna see the guy, it's in his rig.

> MARLENE *enters, wearing her uniform. She has her make-up kit and a small, stand-up mirror. She sets up at the kitchen table to do her hair and make-up.*

18

MARLENE:

Well, you didn't have to go on those hauls if you did-
n't want to. Is how I see it.

JIMMY looks to MARLENE until she glances his way.

JIMMY:

Didn't want to? Didn't want to, Marlene? A guy would
have to be a fool not to wanna go on those hauls—
those hauls are the highlight of my life! (*pause*) Okay,
sure the man tends to run behind from time to time
and I have to miss the odd hockey game—but how
many of my friends get to ride in a truck higher'n any
ole building we got around here? You know there's
not a truck stop here to California don't know my
dad? The kinda life that guy has lived?—well, it's no
use even tryna explain it to you, not gonna
understand, no girl could, but the life of a trucker,
and I mean I bin there and I know, it's better
education than anything you learn in school.

MARLENE:

Now who is that I'm hearin' talkin', your dad all over
again.

JIMMY:

(*looking out the back door*) Gives me a chance to get outa
here, see for myself there's somethin' besides nothin'
out some people's windows. Nothin', that's what I
gotta look at. We live smack dab in the middle of
nowhere—correction, the Canadian side of nowhere.
Houses 'at were here're long gone, fillin' station's history, and us?—we're sittin' in this café like we're stuck
in the muck.

MARLENE:

Your shirt's ironed, it's on the back of my doorknob.

JIMMY:

We should get one of those big tractor-trailers and haul this unit outa here, straight into town. Where we can at least be part of life. This—this is the last thing a Canadian sees when he leaves home and the first thing an American sees when he arrives.

MARLENE:

Hey. Never mind. Gonna be changes. Big ones. Just soon's I get the money.

JIMMY:

Gonna Scotch-tape the rips in the leatherette out there, is that it?

MARLENE:

Gonna put a decent bathroom in there. (*motioning to the back suite*) Gonna have a bathtub and a shower, and I'm gonna do it all up in pink. And that's gonna be the end of goin' out to the farm for a bath. Or standin' in that aluminum box we got now. Gonna get chiffon curtains. Priscillas. Gonna have it lookin' just like the magazines, so just you wait.

> *Pause.*

JIMMY:

Mum, I got the money. I'll do it for ya. I got the money in my account right now, I saved a lot this summer, we can getcha a pink bathtub—

MARLENE:

Don't want a pink bathtub, want a white one, want pink accessories, I want floral design, I want wallpaper, I want it exactly how I got it in my mind and I'm not lettin' you pay for it, I can afford it, I'm just waitin' 'til—

JIMMY:

Oh waitin', waitin', waitin'—for what?!—him to come back to you? (*He freezes. He shoves the screen door open, and stands out back.*) How could I say that to her? How?

MARLENE:

Yeah, well I got somethin' to say to you, too.

JIMMY:

(*re-enters*) I'll tell you how—it's—it's him comin' out in me, it's my dad, just like you said.

MARLENE:

Nice try but no go.

JIMMY:

I know you wouldn't take him back, I know that—even if he come crawlin'.

MARLENE:

Which he did more'n once.

JIMMY:

He's nothin' but a good ole boy, never be no more.

MARLENE:

That's right.

JIMMY:

Even if he just got married.

> Pause. The sound of the combine. JIMMY looks outside.

MARLENE:

Jimmy.

JIMMY:

Why does he always have to have a haul up to Canada when Grandad needs me the most? Talk about inconsideration. People, they got no respect for the farmer in this world.

MARLENE:

Never mind the world, just let me say.

JIMMY:

I should be allowed to have your car today, or
Maxine's truck, roar into school, register like a
madman, then race my tail back out to the field. Stay
at 'er 'til I drop, like Grandad does. But no, me, I
sleep in, mouth off, and let Grandad talk me into
havin' Friday off. Frost is gonna nail our crop but
good and I was gonna kick around the Doughnut
Hole all day? (*The combine fades.*) Which now I can't do
'cause my dad's comin' up?

The sound of a pick-up truck stopping.

MARLENE:

Now here's your grandma's truck, act normal.

JIMMY:

Well how 'bout tellin' me if I'm comin' or goin'
Marlene?

MARLENE:

And you can quit callin' me Marlene.

JIMMY:

I call Maxine Maxine.

MARLENE:

Maxine's Maxine, I'm me.

JIMMY:

You call her Maxine.

MARLENE:

She's my mother.

JIMMY:

And you're my mother.

MARLENE:

Way you talk to me I'd never know it.

JIMMY:

Just tell me what to do.

MARLENE:

　Fine.

JIMMY:

　Fine I tell Dad I got the crop to get off?

MARLENE:

　Well, you could.

JIMMY:

　Or fine I tell Grandad my dad's—

MARLENE:

　Get a move on, you're seventeen and you shouldn't
　have to be told—

JIMMY:

　Told what?

MARLENE:

　And when I was seventeen I had you.

JIMMY:

　Yeah? Well, now I'm seventeen and I got you.

MARLENE:

　You got me?—I wish I had me when I was your age, I
　wish I had a mother tellin' me not to go—

JIMMY:

　On a haul?

MARLENE:

　It's not a haul he was callin' about, it's not a haul he's
　got in mind.

JIMMY:

　Well what?

MARLENE:

　He wants you to go live down there! With him! And
　her! In a brand new house! Happy?

JIMMY:

　Huh?

MARLENE:

Now go get washed for school!

JIMMY:

School?

MARLENE:

If you're goin'!

JIMMY:

Goin'!

MARLENE:

I mean it!

JIMMY:

What?

> *MAXINE flings open the back door. She's wearing a windbreaker over her uniform. She throws her purse down.*

MAXINE:

Hey! Shut your battletraps! Can hear ya all in the parkin' lot.

> *JIMMY exits to the front.*

MARLENE:

Jimmy—

MAXINE:

Never mind the parkin' lot, they can hear ya in Missoura. And way up in Yellowknife, for that matter—suppose the coffee's not bin turned on? Wait for Maxine to do it, why not. (*MAXINE prepares the drip machine. MARLENE starts to follow JIMMY, then stops.*) After she's listened to the "Rock of Ages" all night long. Comin' outa your dad's nasal passages—spent half the night on the sofa—then he wonders why I sleep over here so much—gimme one your cigarettes, I'm out.

MARLENE:

Just got Canadian. Coupla Lucky's in the junk drawer.

> *MAXINE opens the drawer, gets a cigarette, takes the lighter out of her brassiere, and lights up. MARLENE lights up another of hers.*

MAXINE:

Well, I'll tell ya.

MARLENE:

That couldn't've bin handled worse.

MAXINE:

Those people in Oklahoma never cease to amaze me.

MARLENE:

Is Dad comin' in for breakfast?

MAXINE:

Yeah, this one of 'em got herself on Good Mornin' America for winnin' too many toaster ovens, huh.

MARLENE:

(*looking out the back*) I should go runnin' out there.

MAXINE:

Give a guess how many.

MARLENE:

Nine.

MAXINE:

Nine nothin', that squirrel won seven hundred and eighty-three.

MARLENE:

What's this we're talkin'?

MAXINE:

Those deals your Aunt Thelma uses for that asparagus effort she shoves atcha and calls a meal. "When's the last time you folks sat down together nice like this?" —far as I'm concerned that woman as good as killed

your Uncle Carl with too many minced baloney
sandwiches.

MARLENE:

Jimmy! (*to MAXINE*) I don't know how you can be so
like that to Dad's family and sweet as pie to any
stranger't come in here.

JIMMY:

(*comes to the order window*) What?

MARLENE:

I—I forget now, never mind.

MAXINE:

I had a fourth cousin from Oklahoma.

MARLENE:

(*to JIMMY*) Our own's free back there, why you usin'
the Men's?

JIMMY:

Just like that, up and go?

MAXINE:

He was so fat when he died they had to knock out the
livin' room window to get his casket out.

JIMMY:

Mum.

MARLENE:

All I need now is that fat casket story.

MAXINE:

That's no lie, his name was Dalton Dooey.

JIMMY:

Mum.

MAXINE:

Or not Dalton neither, Barney.

MARLENE:

(*to JIMMY*) What?

MAXINE:

Barney Dalton.

JIMMY:

Just like that, I said.

MARLENE:

If that's what you want.

MAXINE:

I got a black and white snapshot o' that casket comin' out the window, don't ask me where.

JIMMY:

You weren't even gonna let me in on it, it just come out by chance.

MARLENE:

I was tellin' you all along.

JIMMY:

You weren't tellin' me anything but to get washed.

MAXINE:

My aunt Marietta was there in full force and she weighed a good three hundred herself.

MARLENE:

Didn't I say our own's free, why you usin' the Men's?

JIMMY:

You were in it when I started out goin' and I'd like to know why you called me out here in the first place.

MARLENE:

I didn't mean to.

MAXINE:

You kids don't care but that cousin holds the State record down there. He sure does.

JIMMY:

For what, Maxine?

MAXINE:

Fat.

MARLENE:

Mum.

MAXINE:

State o' Oklahoma!—Look it up.

MARLENE:

Where's a person look that up?

MAXINE:

This is it.

> *JIMMY exits from the order window. MAXINE has begun her morning preparations—getting the food out and ready, garnishes arranged, etc. She continues speaking through the order window.*

MAXINE:

Put Waylon on!

MARLENE:

Never mind Waylon, is your grill on?

MAXINE:

(*singing*) "I'd rather be an Okie from Muskokie—"

MARLENE:

That's Merle Haggard's song, Maxine.

MAXINE:

He did time, Merle did.

MARLENE:

I'm askin' you not to sing.

MAXINE:

(*singing*) "Where they still fly Old Glory down on Main Street."

MARLENE:

I'll pay ya to stop. In American funds.

The sound of the combine. MARLENE looks out back. She goes out the door, she comes back in.

MARLENE:
Why aren't I knowin' what to do?

MAXINE:
(*still with her preparations*) 'Course the farther south you go the fatter people get.

MARLENE:
Mum, can you please just not say nothin' for awhile?

MAXINE:
How come? And why aren't I being let in on it?

Pause.

MARLENE:
On what?

MAXINE:
On round number nine hundred and forty-two you were havin' with that kid.

MARLENE:
Don't make it sound like I've done nothin' but fight with him—

MAXINE:
These walls tell the story, I'm not sayin' anything original—and as far as that other goes, call me a liar but people from, say, Kansas south, are nine out of ten of 'em that come in here full-fledged porkers. It's the way they eat down there, solid lard casseroles. My mother? She looked like a size four knittin' needle towards the end, sure, but she was a pudgeball when she was young, she didn't lose that weight 'til she left Texas. Minnesota thinned my mother right down. What you havin' for breakfast, I'm gonna go for a bacon sandwich.

The sound of a tanker. MAXINE throws a slab of bacon onto the grill.

MARLENE:

I'll eat with Dad, I guess.

MAXINE:

So I tried to call over to wake yas up but you were on the line.

MARLENE:

Who was I talkin' to, Mum?

MAXINE:

Not me, I couldn't get through.

MARLENE:

How long you listen in on that party line?

MAXINE:

Hey, I got no time for sweet talk before my mornin' coffee. Which don't pose a threat to your dad. Last time anything nice found its way outa his mouth was when you were born. "Well done," he says, like I just baked a cake.

MARLENE:

So you don't know what Don said?

MAXINE:

What does he ever say? Comin' to get the kid for a haul, isn't he?—Only boy in the world hasn't seen the left hand side of his father, just the right—steering. Oh yeah, speakin' o' steering—I think Jimmy should have your car today, first day and all.

MARLENE:

Wrecked his truck, should have my car?

MAXINE:

Okay, how 'bout my truck then?

MARLENE:

Mum, I already said no to him.

MAXINE:

You're takin' this little tumble in the ditch too far. So the kid had a bottle o' beer and hit the only vertical object in a hundred mile radius. As if you never done nothin' dumb when you were that age.

MARLENE:

Never wrecked a truck, I'll tell ya.

MAXINE:

That's 'cause you left home before you were old enough to reach the gas pedal. You put me through my paces, don't kid yourself. Fifteen years old and that sonovagun strolls in here like Johnny Cash, charms the daylights outa you and me both.

MARLENE:

Okay, fine, never mind.

MAXINE:

Gets herself married and taken down to Wyoming, set up in the trailer park, starin' at those narrow walls six outa seven.

MARLENE:

Don't tell me about that seventh day, Mum.

MAXINE:

Which was all it took.

MARLENE:

And now we're into the grilled cheese.

MAXINE:

I'm standin' at my grill slappin' my cheese together and who pulls up but Don and Marlene in that ole rig—dumps her off here like a sac' o' potatoes and she's showin' this far out.

MARLENE:

I wasn't that far "a-out" and I don't appreciate talk like that in this café, I just don't this mornin'.

MAXINE:

And you can't blame me because your dad tried to warn you, he seen through Don right from the time that blizzard holed Don up here.

MARLENE:

Finished?

MAXINE:

Point is you weren't an easy kid to raise, I think Jimmy should take my truck.

MARLENE gathers her make-up and mirror and curling iron and heads to the back.

MARLENE:

Jimmy does somethin' wrong it's me who puts her through her paces.

MAXINE:

He works hard, Mar.

MARLENE:

You're sayin' I've been too strict? Well, that's on my conscience from now 'til Kingdom Come 'cept for everyone tells me I'm not strict enough and just 'cause I—I say no doesn't mean I always mean it. Bad enough I ground the kid and then pretend I didn't every time he wants to go out—who ever heard of groundin' a kid only when he's home?—okay, so to make up for it I should let him take your truck to school, he's suffered enough.

MAXINE:

Well, he has.

MARLENE:

What's it matter now anyway?

MAXINE:

These are my sin'imen's exactly. (*watches MARLENE*)
Com'ere, honey. (*MARLENE doesn't move. MAXINE goes to
her.*) Kids, you know, they want a firm hand when it
comes right down to it. They know what's good for
'em. Me, I raised you not knowin' half the time if I was
doin' the right thing. Far as that-all goes my mom
barely looked up from her gin-rummy the day I set the
prairie on fire. Scooter and me burnt away half the
state o' Minnesota smokin' roll-me-owns and you
wanna know what Mom did?—sent us to the movies. I
fixed her, I went ahead and turned out normal. Which
boils down to the same thing—you're a darn good
mother, quit worryin'.

MARLENE:

Was I really, Mum?

MAXINE:

(*going to the grill*) Sure, why not?

MARLENE:

'Cause I really need to—to hear that right now.

MAXINE:

(*coming back*) Why?—I say somethin' wrong again?—I
did, darn it—well, I didn't mean nothin' about all that
other, runnin' off to Wyoming, you were a good kid,
prat'ly raised yourself, don't pay Maxine any mind,
this is just me and my dumb self.

MARLENE:

No Mum, it's me—I'm touchy today, that's all.

MAXINE:

(*taking her into her arms*) Aw, honey. What else is new?

MARLENE:

Pardon?

MAXINE:

You kinda got the market cornered on bein' touchy, let's face it but how 'bout some ham an' eggs, huh?

MARLENE:

You think I'm touchy? Well, I'm not touchy, I'm not the least bit touchy. (*re-gathers her things to take into the back*) Every time Don calls he's comin' up I get my life dragged up and made out like all I had with him was bad times—well, Max?—there was plenny o' good times down in Wyoming that you don't know about, neither of you two, Jimmy or you. And I'd definitely appreciate it if you'd—because my marriage wasn't a total joke even though my life is right now for the very simple reason that I darn well know how to have a good time and I'm gonna start one o' these days and boy. Okay? Well, I got pictures in this back suite in four different photo albums, provin' I had good times in Wyoming.

MAXINE:

Oh, hey!—Jimmy!—You gotta get your pitcher taken, first day o' school!

MARLENE:

(*exiting to the back and returning*) Wanna know a good time, I'll tell you a good time and it was a gas. Don took me to a county fair down there. He won every teddy bear that fella had. Tossin' baseballs in a basket. I was sixteen. Well, didn't those darn teddy bears fill the back seat o' that Chevrolet. That is no exaggeration. It was a fun.

MAXINE:

Oh, there's no doubt in my mind, back home in Minnesota we had fairs bigger'n anything you'd ever find up here.

MARLENE:

    I left forty, fifty bears back in Wyoming.

MAXINE:

    (*doing her garnishes*) Bigger'n the ones in Wyoming, our fairs.

MARLENE:

    Mum, you never bin to Wyoming, least of all a fair. All those teddy bears and enough *Screen Gem* magazines to sink a ship, I lef' back there.

MAXINE:

    Jimmy-Jim!

MARLENE:

    I only brung one o' those bears back home—shoved it into that ole trunk at the las' minute—'member you gimme that old trunk to take down?—well, that bear? That bear become Jimmy's Floppy.

JIMMY:

    (*entering from the front*) What year have we time lapsed into now?

MAXINE:

    (*to JIMMY*) That trunk weren't mine to give if the truth were known.

MARLENE:

    Nothin', get dressed.

MAXINE:

    I snafoofled that trunk off my Aunt Lizzie and she come up the Mississippi River on nothin' but charm.

JIMMY:

    You mean that old bear I used to practice my slaps with?

MAXINE:

    She was from Baton Rouge, Louisiana, Lizzie was.

MARLENE:

Well, your dad won me that bear.

MAXINE:

She dyed her hair red and it turned green.

JIMMY:

Dad did?

MARLENE:

Your dad could throw a ball.

MAXINE:

All Americans can, they're the best baseball players in the United States, 'er the world—I was lead pitcher for my team, that's how good I was.

JIMMY:

Geez, Mum, I—

MAXINE:

I played for a soda jerk league.

MARLENE:

(*to JIMMY*) You what?

MAXINE:

Me and eighteen soda jerks.

MARLENE:

No, Mum—

MAXINE:

I wasn't ever a soda jerk, I just played with 'em.

MARLENE:

Jimmy's tryna talk.

MAXINE:

But the café I waitressed was right across the street from the drugstore and me and this jerk got talkin' one day and before he knew it I was on his team.

JIMMY:

No, I was just gonna say I wouldn'na minded seein' Dad—well, seein' him win you that ... bear. (*exits to the back suite*)

MARLENE:

Yeah?

MAXINE:

Oh yeah, we had a ball, and as I say, that trunk has a bit o' history all right. (*pause*) 'Course so did Lizzie.

MARLENE:

Mum.

MAXINE:

Why do you think she headed north?—the weather?

MARLENE:

Jimmy wishes he coulda seen his dad and me at that fair.

MAXINE:

Oh, it was somethin' all right.

MARLENE:

Mum, you weren't there.

MAXINE:

I weren't there?

MARLENE:

You were standin' right here slappin' your cheese together waitin' for me to show up pregnant, remember.

MAXINE:

Yeah, well, you got that right.

MARLENE:

And he didn't drop me off like a "sac' o' potatoes," either—it was my choice to come back up here, to have my baby north o' that border.

MAXINE:

I don't know how I always end up touchin' off these Canadian nerves.

MARLENE:

And things would be a whole lot smoother around here if you'd quit callin' anything out the ordinary Canadian.

MAXINE:

Well, fine, but where's the camera?

MARLENE:

And Don come by quite a bit at first, we had a normal marriage off'n on those few times—

MAXINE:

First one in the family to get his grade twelve, I'm capturin' it on Kodak.

MARLENE:

Okay, so maybe I wasn't a perfect mother, sue me.

MAXINE:

It's not in here.

MARLENE:

And Don was always showin' up with somethin' for that kid—

MAXINE:

Hey, Jimmy!

MARLENE:

Droppin' fifty dollars just like that—

MAXINE:

It was in this drawer.

MARLENE:

That dirt bike alone and top o' the line tanker toys, those don't come cheap and Mum if I go over there and find that camera?

MAXINE:

Jimmy, run out to the farm and look for the Instamatic!

MARLENE:

I know I haven't—I'm not—and Don's not either but when you're not together it's hard to be alone raisin' a kid and Mum it's right here starin' you in the face.

MAXINE:

I can't see for lookin', never could.

MARLENE:

That's because you don't keep things in order, I clean this drawer out one day and you're messin' it up the next and I happen to have a bone to pick with you about this very sort o' thing—you were in my unicorn collection yesterday, it was not how I lef' it and you better come clean right now, Max.

MAXINE:

(*exiting back*) Found it, Jimmy—never mind!

MARLENE:

Right now, Maxine—I mean it, you come marching back right here and you—and—Dad—!

JIM has entered from outside. He takes off his hat.
MARLENE turns quickly around to face him.

JIM:

Uh huh.

MARLENE:

Dad, I—Don called!

JIM:

Oh yeah.

MARLENE:

He—wants Jimmy, he wants him to go live down in Wyoming—this is what he says to me on that phone.

Pause.

JIM:

In Wyoming, eh.

MARLENE:

Live with him and his new wife. (*pause*) Linda.

JIM:

Oh yeah.

MARLENE:

Why didn't I just grab the Mathison place when it was offered?—I had the down payment. But no, I raise the kid here—raise? I didn't even raise him, he just all of a sudden got big and now he's leavin'—he's leavin', Dad.

JIM:

All right, simmer down.

MARLENE:

Don'll be here at four.

JIM:

Number one, he won't be on time. Number two, Jimmy's not moving into that old trailer house o' Don's.

MARLENE:

Oh no Dad, a trailer's not good enough for this gal— Don bought her a brand new house.

Pause.

JIM:

Have you told Jimmy yet?

MARLENE:

Sets her up nice—second wife gets what the first wife wants, it's a fact o' life, it's in all the magazines.

JIM:

Jimmy, he know yet Marlene?

MARLENE:

Oh, you know me Dad, I decide to turn the jukebox on, I make his bed like my life depends on it, I end up yellin' it out to him like it was all his fault.

JIM:

Oh Marlene.

MARLENE:

I know. Dad, please—please will you—so that he knows and everything like that?

Pause.

JIM:

Well, I will Marlene, I'll talk to him for you. But don't you think he'd—

MARLENE:

Yes, I do think he'd rather hear it from me. But I can't talk to that kid, I never could, and you know that.

JIM:

Yes, I do.

Pause.

MARLENE:

What're you gonna say, so I know?

JIM:

Why don't we all three of us sit down here at the table and more or less iron this out together?

MARLENE:

Okay, that'd be good I guess.

JIM:

I take it you haven't told your mother.

MARLENE:

No.

JIM:

Let's do ourselves a favour and keep it that way.

JIM heads to the back, rolling up his sleeves to wash.

MARLENE:

Dad?

JIM:

Eh?

MAXINE:

(*enters carrying the camera*) Yeah, you get washed Jim and you can be in the pitcher.

JIM:

You're not takin' my picture.

JIMMY:

(*entering*) Grandad.

JIM:

(*as he exits*) Jimmy.

> *JIMMY looks after JIM.*

MAXINE:

Isn't he handsome in that shirt, he's gonna have a swarm o' girls around him today.

JIMMY:

Swarm. Right. (*He allows himself to be shuffled out the back door by MAXINE. She barely aims the camera in the right direction before snapping. JIMMY comes inside to sit at the table.*) Only guy in the hemisphere has to have little snaps of his first days of school pinned up over the till for everyone to gawk at.

MAXINE:

Never you mind, you get your grade twelve and you and me are gonna get in my pick-up and head 'er south.

JIMMY:

Mum?

MARLENE:

Yeah?

MAXINE:

(*going to pour coffee*) We'll see every state in the union.

*The sound of the door opening and closing out front.
MARLENE glances towards it.*

MARLENE:

I said, yeah.

MAXINE:

And get a souvenir spoon.

JIMMY:

Forget it.

*MARLENE takes the coffee pot and menus and heads to
the front. MAXINE looks to JIMMY. He gets up and goes
toward the front, stopping. He goes back to the table.*

MAXINE:

Hey Sport.

JIMMY:

Yeah?

MAXINE:

Tell your Max what's wrong.

JIMMY:

Can't.

MAXINE:

Yes you can, you can tell your Max everything.

JIMMY:

She don't care.

MAXINE:

About what? Don't she care. Huh?

Pause.

JIMMY:

I get in her way around here, okay. I'm far too large.
For my body. That kinda thing. Not only that but I'm a
total clutz-act on the farm, I'm a zero-winner, an A-one
loser—Grandad's always havin' to come bail me out,
make me feel small. Does he ever say anything? No.
He just … stares. If he'd only haul off and lose his
temper, just once. Why can't he yell at me or throw
the hammer down or spit even? Why Max?

MAXINE:

He's weird. They both of 'em are, your mother and
him. It's that side o' the family, somethin' in the
blood—which if you were to ask her royal highness
mother-in-law over there she'd claim was blue. Take
your Aunt Thelma and that washtub of curdled jello
she tries to peddle off as dessert for those goldarn
picnics of hers—with that strain of perversion floatin'
around in the family?—well you're bound to be a little
backward Jimmy—but hey, you and me, we'll show
'em—we're gonna leave the whole silly lot of 'em up
here huddled around their hot water bottles and we're
gonna see America—from L.A. to New York, zig-zag-
gin' our way down to the South—the Virginias, the
Carolinas—oh, you name it—we'll go see where
President Kennedy was buried and Bobby o' course
and up to Yankee Stadium—

JIMMY:

Yeah, and I wanna see the Yankees and the Mets and
the Islanders and the Rangers—

MAXINE:

You ain't just a-whistlin' Dixie, kid—we'll see it all and
sidestep over to Minnesota so you can see where your
Max was born and where she'll be laid to rest when
she cashes out for the last time.

JIMMY:

You're gettin' buried up here, aren't you?

MAXINE:

I'm gettin' buried in American soil!

JIMMY:

But what about Grandad?

MAXINE:

He can darn well come down there—if you think I'm gonna be a hop, skip and a jump from her majesty and all this crew up here—if any of 'em ever do us the favour of passin' away—

JIMMY:

Wait a minute Max, you and Grandad aren't hardly together now—don't you at least wanna be together in the end?

MAXINE:

Only one in the family I took a half-likin' to was the old man and he had to be the first one to go. Mind you, it took eleven operations—and your grandad and I are together now, what're you talkin' about?

JIMMY:

You're not, Max. Last night was the first time in over a week you didn't sleep here.

MAXINE:

You don't like your Max stayin' overnight?

JIMMY:

No, I do—I do Max, but Grandad needs you over there.

MAXINE:

Oh, he don't need no one.

> *JIM comes in from the back suite but JIMMY has his back to him and cannot see.*

JIMMY:

Yeah, he does. 'Cause ya see, a man like Grandad—
well, any man—they like to have someone, Max. It's
time you understood that about men. That's how we
are—they are—they need the security. The emotional
security.

MAXINE:

That right, Jim?

JIMMY:

(*jumping up*) Grandad!—Geez, Max—you coulda said
somethin'—

JIM takes his place at the table.

MAXINE:

Yeah, but uh, a woman—you figger she don't need
this here security, is that it?

JIM:

Leave the boy.

MAXINE:

Huh Jimmy?

Pause.

JIMMY:

Women got it built-in as far as I can tell. So if he needs
it and she's got it, she should provide him with it, and
stay put.

JIM:

Pass the milk.

MAXINE:

(*going to the grill*) Grandad wouldn't touch that one
with a ten-foot pole, huh Jim?

JIM:

Right.

MAXINE:

He may be slow but he's not stupid.

JIM:

(*to JIMMY*) Time you get to bed?

JIMMY:

Not sure.

JIM:

Told you to come in off the field by 11:30. It was nowhere near 11:30 time you done all that.

JIMMY:

I—I don't need sleep today, it's just Registration.

MAXINE:

I never slep' when I was his age, I partied all night and worked a double-shift to boot—kid's got my stamina, don'tcha Jimmy?

JIMMY:

Yep.

MAXINE:

What's the capital of Tennessee?

JIM:

Not now, Maxine.

MAXINE:

We're goin' to Nashville next year, do that place up right, huh Jimmy-Jim?

JIM:

Can your mother see you a minute when her order's done?

MAXINE:

Where was Lincoln hung?

JIMMY:

He wasn't hung, he was shot.

MAXINE:

That's what I meant, shot.

JIMMY:

(*to JIM*) See me about what, she tell ya?

JIM:

She told me. And I understand she told you, too.

MAXINE:

Where was Lincoln shot then?

JIM:

Though not in the best way, perhaps. See Jimmy, your mother—

MAXINE:

Where was Lincoln shot!

JIM:

(*to JIMMY*) Just tell your grandmother where Lincoln was shot.

JIMMY:

Oh—he was shot—uh, was it Edmonton they got ole Lincoln?

> *Pause. JIMMY signals to JIM to play along.*

JIM:

Butte, Montana. Custer'd nailed him.

JIMMY:

Was it Custer Grandad?—or Louis Riel?

MAXINE:

Who?

JIM:

Got me there, Jimmy.

JIMMY:

We give up, Max—where was Lincoln shot?

MAXINE:

> (*pointing outside*) Out by that burnin' barrel for all you two care. Well fine, but it's a cryin' shame these kids don't know their American history. Sittin' on the most powerful nation in the world and all they wanna do is play hockey.

JIMMY:

> We know more about you than you know about us.

MAXINE:

> We?—us?—Hey!—you're more American than you are Canadian!—and I know my Canadian history!—what there is of it. But I don't forget my American ruts, and you don't neither.

MARLENE:

> (*entering from the front*) A daily over.

MAXINE:

> If it wasn't for me you'd know zip about your ruts—capital Zee-I-P.

JIMMY:

> My what?

MAXINE:

> Ruts, ruts, where ya come from.

JIMMY:

> I think she means roots, doesn't she Grandad?

MAXINE:

> I said ruts.

JIMMY:

> Spell that zip again, Max—was that Zed-I-P?

MARLENE:

> Daily over, eh Mum.

MAXINE:

>(*to MARLENE*) And as for you, that ole trunk o' Lizzie's?
>It was a darn sight more full up when you took it down
>to Wyoming than it was when I brung it up from
>Minnesota, wasn't it Jim. Yes, it was. I come up to this
>country with what the little boy shot at and missed,
>that's how I started out my married life—didn't I Jim?
>Yes I did.

JIM:

>Sit down, Marlene.

MAXINE:

>And I packed that ole trunk in half an hour.

MARLENE:

>Daily over.

MAXINE:

>Kid has to come to me, an American, to find out how
>this half of him ended up up here—(*to JIMMY*) What's
>Grandad talk to you about when you're milkin' those
>cows every night, huh?

MARLENE:

>Mum, a daily.

MAXINE:

>Huh?

JIMMY:

>I don't know.

MARLENE:

>Daily, Mum, daily.

JIM:

>Usually got the radio on durin' chores.

MAXINE:

>The CBC on in the barn. Most educated cows in the
>county.

JIMMY:

District.

> *MAXINE has finally retreated to the grill area to prepare the order. MARLENE, seated at the table, glances to JIMMY. Then to her dad.*

JIM:

Jimmy?

JIMMY:

Yeah?

JIM:

There's a lot o' people tend to think of life as, well, as a road you go down.

MAXINE:

(*singing*) "Zippity-do-dah, zippity-day."

JIM:

And in that road, there's sometimes the odd fork that comes up.

MAXINE:

"My oh my what a wonderful day."

JIM:

Well today, you've reached one of those forks and your mother here wants you to consider—

MAXINE:

"Plenny o' sunshine, plenny all day—"

JIM:

Maxine?

MAXINE:

"Zippity-do-dah, zippity-day!"—What?

JIM:

A person can't have a decent say.

MAXINE:

Huh?

MARLENE:

Leave her, Dad.

JIMMY:

Leave her.

MAXINE:

(*coming from around the grill*) What? (*Pause. She slithers over to JIM, singing.*) I'm ... in the mood for love. Simply because you're neeeaaarrr me—(*She wraps her arms around JIM, kissing him on the head. He remains motionless.*) Isn't he just the best-lookin', heart-thumpin', sexiest man in this great big bowlin' ball called Earth? Huh Jim?—You handsome brute—huh?—That trip up here with that old trunk on the train?—huh?—'member? (*to MARLENE*) Four pillow slips is about all I had.

MARLENE:

Mum, that fellow looked in a hurry.

MAXINE:

I was nineteen and you think you were dumb when you got married, Marlene?—I was dumb—I was waitin' tables in this coffee shop and as I say, in walks Jim and his buddy—well, I give a look to Margaret—she's since died—and I says to her, "Kiddo?—I'll give ya my four-some if you gimme that deuce!"—and didn't Jim and his buddy end up draggin' that order on for the better part of an afternoon, huh Jim?

JIM:

Unlike the fellow out front here that wants his filled now so he can be on his way.

MAXINE:

They were down in Minnesota for a big auction huh, well, it weren't often you met a fella with manners so I married him.

JIM:

> (*to MARLENE*) Tell the gentleman it won't be long.

> *MARLENE doesn't. She knows JIM is just embarrassed.*

MAXINE:

> I took him home to meet my folks and my mom was
> sold on him before he hit the livin' room—took his
> shoes off at the door! Didn't you, Jim?

JIM:

> May have.

MAXINE:

> He did.

MARLENE:

> The daily over, Mum.

MAXINE:

> Well, my dad he'd just as soon get rid o' me as have
> me stay on account of the fact me and Mom fought so
> terrible and her with that horrible accent, I mean she
> never shut up from mornin' 'til night, you talk about a
> screen door in a wind storm, that woman never quit.
> Pop, he says,—I can hear him to this day—"Well"—he
> was from down Iowa way—"They-all up in Canada,
> they did join the War before we did"—hands us
> sixteen dollars and we were married by four o'clock.
> Right, Jim?

JIM:

> It seemed like longer. (*pause*) If I were that gentleman
> out there I'd have second thoughts about returning to
> this place with the service so slow.

MAXINE:

> (*to MARLENE*) That slop pail there's got more romance
> in him than your dad does. (*getting to work*) Prob'ly
> doesn't even remember meetin' me. Then he has the

nerve to take exception if some fella in here pays attention to me.

JIM:

I pay attention to you every time you wanted me to I wouldn't have the crop in, never mind off.

MAXINE goes to fill the order—bacon, eggs, hash browns, toast—as JIM takes a serviette, and MARLENE begins to clear the table.

JIM:

And it's not that they pay attention to her, it's that she pays attention to them. Marlene, leave the dishes.

MARLENE sits down. A tanker is heard going by.

JIM:

As I was saying.

Pause.

JIMMY:

(*jumping up*) I know the crop's not off, I know I'm holdin' you up.

JIM stares at JIMMY for a long time. JIMMY sits down.

JIM:

Let's just put our cards on the table. Now Don, he tells us he's got a—a wife now, a house, and he's ready to have a son. Well, that's handy, considering his son is soon celebrating his eighteenth birthday.

JIMMY:

Why is it my fault I'm eighteen too soon?—I can't help it he wasn't ready 'til now—

MARLENE:

You're sayin' it's my fault?

JIM:

Wait a second—

JIMMY:

Did I say it was yours, Marlene?

MARLENE:

Well, I know that bedspread's for a little boy, I so much as said it was already.

JIM:

Bedspread?

MARLENE:

I see those plaid spreads every time I flip through that Sears catalogue, but do I order one?

JIM:

Let's keep our eye on the ball.

MARLENE:

Red and black, green and black, yellow and black, I can't decide, I don't order one.

JIMMY:

I don't want a bedspread.

MARLENE:

I shoulda got him a VCR.

JIMMY:

VCR?

JIM:

Now how would that have solved a darn thing?

JIMMY:

I got my own money.

MARLENE:

I know I made you work till soon's you were old enough to reach it, I know I made you save your money.

JIMMY:

I didn't mind working till.

MARLENE:

Yes, you did.

JIMMY:

No, I didn't.

MARLENE:

You hated working till.

JIMMY:

I loved working till.

MARLENE:

Hated.

JIMMY:

Loved. (*exits into the back*)

MARLENE:

(*looks to JIM*) Dad—I—go after him.

MAXINE:

(*through the order window*) So where ya from, buddy?

JIM:

Jimmy?

MAXINE:

Texas!—My mother was from Texas!

JIM:

Why couldn't he've bin from Saskatchewan?

MAXINE:

Lubbock!—You're from Lubbock? (*heading around to the front*) Well, my mother was from Amarillo!

MARLENE:

You saw what happened, Dad—you saw what I did— I'm gettin' outa here, I'm headin' down that highway, I'm not bein' heard from again.

JIM:

Marlene.

MARLENE:

I'm thirty-four and I'm nowhere. (*pause*) My life's over, my kid's leavin'. I got nothin' keepin' me here.

JIM:

You got a café to run for starters.

MARLENE:

What I got it burns down? I got grade nine. Jimmy's gone farther'n me and in more ways'n one. What's he want from me when he's the one bin carted all over the western part o' the United States? Knows Texas like the back' his hand—me, I bin to a trailer park in Wyoming and the Woolco Mall in Lethbridge—I'm the one should be askin' him what to do.

JIM:

When it come right down to it you're still his mother.

MARLENE:

I know that and it's about time he grew up and realized it. He's seventeen and—oh, what am I sayin', seventeen isn't very old, it just isn't old enough to leave home.

JIM:

No. I know. Neither was fifteen.

> *MARLENE freezes. Pause. She slowly turns around to look at JIM.*

MAXINE:

(*off*) Flip those eggs, Mar!

> *Automatically MARLENE moves to the grill to attend to the order.*

JIM:

Seemed like one day you were gettin' underfoot in here or beggin' for a ride in the tractor and the next day, it was you that character was comin' to take across the line.

MARLENE:

You can't 'member that.

JIM:

Eh?

MARLENE:

You were combinin'. You didn't come in off the field to say—say good-bye.

JIM:

You knew why that was.

> *Pause.*

MARLENE:

Had an idea. Guess I got a better one right now. (*as she sets the order up on the ledge*) Wanna know the first thing to come to me when I hung up that phone this morning?—It was like Jimmy was eleven years old comin' in the door there. All summer long I figgered I was teachin' him how to earn a dollar—oh, he had to have those Cooperalls and me I couldn't see shellin' out a hundert bucks for hockey pants when his last year's still had wear. I make him work till his whole summer in addition to the—the farm—his dad shows up end o' August and takes him down to Texas like it were across the road—I'm supposed to compete with that? Kid comes back full of himself, goes into town with that Cooperall money—

JIM:

Okay now.

MARLENE:

Here, what's he do but end up at Regency Jewelers—Margie, she tells me after, she says, "Marlene, your son put that $97.50 down on my counter like he was layin' out his life for you." Why'd he have to see me lookin' in the window at those diamond chip earrings? And what I do when he comes through this door with that velvet box in his hand?

JIM:

He knows—he knows you liked the earrings.

MARLENE:

Not from me showin' it he don't, Dad. (*She looks to the order.*) That order's up and gettin' cold.

> *MAXINE enters talking. She starts to finish the order, realizes that it is up, takes it and is more liberal with the serving and garnishes.*

MAXINE:

(*directing her voice to the front*) Well, if it's your first time up this way, buddy, you better get ready to not know how fast you're driving, how hot it is outside, how hard the wind's blowin' or how much gas you're gettin' for your so-called dollar. As for readin' directions on any box or carton—it's all in the wrist action—you'll see a lot a mode da emploi's—means flip it over to English—wrist action—Canadians got real strong wrists, prepares 'em for hockey careers. (*turning to MARLENE*) Mar, take this to my buddy from Texas—I gotta do my garnishes—(*looking out*) Who me? (*MARLENE takes the order out front.*) No, I'm married. (*MAXINE looks ever so assuredly to JIM for an extended pause. Then she looks back out front through the window as she chops her tomatoes, etc.*) I come up in '49. I was nineteen and dumber 'an a dawg, I married a Canadian boy. He farms just over there. I had about a month o' goin' batty in that farmhouse with Miss High and Mighty mother-in-law and got myself on here—we owned it prat'ly ever since and believe me, buddy, it owns us. My grandson Jimmy? He's an exceptional boy. He could grill a sandwich age o' eight.

MARLENE:

> (*entering*) Mum.

JIM:

> Leave her.

MARLENE:

> She's gonna start in on Jimmy's hockey.

MAXINE:

> He's quite the hockey player—scored a hat trick last year.

MARLENE:

> Watch, she'll show him the puck over the till.

MAXINE:

> We kep' the puck, it's over the till, if you care to take a look.

MARLENE:

> Guess who he sees carryin' on in those stands? Mum. Every goal that kid has scored he has to ask me if I seen it, if I seen the puck go in the net.

MAXINE:

> No, that's not his sister in the picture, that's his mother!—Now she's not married?—Her, she's had her dad wrapped round her little finger since the day I brung her into the world which was in the state o' North Dakota. I didn't wanna have my baby up here, you know what I mean—we were aimin' for Minnesota but we stopped off for coffee in Dakota and I got laughin' so hard I went into labour—didn't I Jim?

JIM:

> I don't think laughing actually brought the baby on.

MARLENE:

> Mum, this fellow I don't know from Sunday now knows how I come into the world.

MAXINE:

Uh huh. (*pause*) You know who you look like standin'
there, don't you? Thelma.

MARLENE:

Thelma. Thelma, Dad!

MAXINE:

With a touch of her majesty mixed in there too, huh
Jim?

MARLENE:

She winked! She thinks it's funny!

JIM:

Let's just bring Jimmy out here.

MAXINE:

Well, I can't understand it—I teach my daughter her
presidents age o' nine, I breathe on her, I spit on my
Kleenex and wipe the Hershey Bar off her face and
what does she turn around and do on me. End up
Canadian.

JIM:

Maybe we should shoot her.

MARLENE:

I don't appreciate bein' told I'm like Aunt Thelma.

MAXINE:

Well, no, why would you, it's not a compliment.

JIM:

Girls.

MARLENE:

And you were in my unicorns yesterday, I know you
were Mum—they were all moved around on that
dresser and you were in them, weren't you. (*looks to
JIM*) Dad?

JIM:

    (*slowly looks to* MAXINE) Were ... you in Marlene's unicorns by any chance?

MAXINE:

    No I wasn't. Just that liver and onions was.

MARLENE:

    That big fat guy was pawin' through my unicorns?

MAXINE:

    Not that liver and onions. The other one with the bad bleach job, her.

MARLENE:

    She brings the bad bleach job into my bedroom.

MAXINE:

    She's from Arkansas.

MARLENE:

    I don't wanna hear about Arkansas.

MAXINE:

    She's bin bottle jobbin' her hair since Marilyn died.

MARLENE:

    I don't wanna hear about Marilyn.

MAXINE:

    I wasn't gonna say nothin' but you asked.

    The sound of the front door.

MARLENE:

    Mum? Can ... you take that new table? And can you top off that Texan's coffee while you're at it?

MAXINE:

    It's 'cause I showed the bad bleach job her unicorns.

MARLENE:

    No, it's not.

MAXINE:

Her luck was down, that gal. Thought I'd perk her up.

MARLENE:

Fine, Mum.

MAXINE:

Her poodle died. (*MARLENE says nothing. MAXINE has taken the menus and moved to the exit.*) Mind you it died in 1964 but are you … mad at your mom?

MARLENE:

Mad at myself, Max.

MAXINE:

(*exiting*) Get over it.

> *JIMMY comes in from the back.*

JIMMY:

Mum?

MARLENE:

What?

JIMMY:

Never mind.

MARLENE:

(*starting to clean*) Got no time for never minds.

JIMMY:

Okay, I need the keys to your car.

MARLENE:

Pardon?

JIMMY:

I gotta go to school one way or the other. If I'm movin' down there I gotta let 'em know, don't I? If I'm stayin' here, I gotta register. So hand 'em over. (*pause*) Hey, no grade twelve will be on that bus. I want you to know that. Just Jimmy. No one else. I'll be the only one. Apart from girls.

MARLENE:

I'm not the one wrecked my truck.

JIMMY:

I have to ride the bus home at four to sit around here
and wait for him, eh?—That's what you want?—Me to
sit around here my only day off?

MARLENE:

No, I—

JIMMY:

Not able to go to hockey conditioning, not able to
even have the dignity of drivin' to school on my first
day o' grade twelve, if I decide to get it?

MARLENE:

Okay, I—

JIMMY:

I'm sorry Grandad!—I know I'm actin' like a brat! So
keep not sayin' nothin', you're warranted.

MARLENE:

Hey, you want a firm hand, you quit makin' it be Dad
and just—just go live down there.

JIM:

Oh Marlene—

MARLENE:

I didn't want him to have that dirt bike, I didn't want
him to grow up spoiled, but his dad shows up here
with a top o' the line model and I'm supposed to
make him take it back?

JIM:

Marlene, sit down.

JIMMY:

Dirt bike?

MARLENE:

And if you're not gettin' your Canadian grade twelve you better darn well get your American!

JIMMY:

I'm not gettin' my American grade twelve, I'm gonna drive truck!

MARLENE:

You're doin' what I tell you to!

JIMMY:

Well, if I could figger out what that is we'll both know!

MARLENE:

Keep your voice down in this café!—Look how I'm talkin' to him, Dad—(*glancing to the front at the sound of the door*) There, another table just walked in, satisfied?—and Mum's tellin' my life history to the other one, and that daily over from Texas is takin' it all in.

JIMMY:

Grandad—

MARLENE:

Not a whole lot I can do about it either.

JIMMY:

She needs a holiday.

MARLENE:

She? Who's she—the cat's mother? This is how that kid talks to me, like we're not even related, like we're brother and sister, you heard the man.

MAXINE:

(*entering*) The Mormon Tabernacle Choir looks like it just walked in and that couple? They're from Edmonton, they seen Wayne Gretzky buyin' a pair o' shoes. In 1984. (*pause*) Grey ones. They both want one my cin'min buns. (*goes to the grill*) So don't mind me, I just work here.

> *The sound of the school bus is heard.* MARLENE *hears it first.*

MARLENE:
There's the bus here. (*JIMMY goes to grab his jean jacket from his room.*) What do you care if the bus is here if you're takin' Max's truck?

> *JIMMY stops.* MAXINE *comes from behind the grill.*

JIMMY:
I'm takin' Max's truck?

MARLENE:
I never said that.

JIMMY:
Yes, you did.

MARLENE:
I did not.

JIMMY:
Yes, you did.

MARLENE:
I did not.

JIMMY:
I think you did.

MARLENE:
I said *if.*

MAXINE:
Hey, get while the gettin's good—(*She takes the keys out of her bra and tosses them to* JIMMY.)—and keep your tail outa the ditch, huh.

MARLENE:
I didn't say he could have it, I said *if.*

JIMMY:

Well, then do I?

MARLENE:

You roll your truck and get handed over Max's keys?

JIMMY:

I didn't expect to.

MARLENE:

What I say don't count.

JIMMY:

What did you say?

MARLENE:

I said *if* I said.

JIMMY:

Let's just get that straight.

MARLENE:

If you're takin' Max's truck, I said!

JIMMY:

So now I can't?

MARLENE:

I didn't say that.

JIMMY:

Yes, you did.

MARLENE:

No I didn't.

JIMMY:

Yes, you did.

MARLENE:

No, I didn't.

The sound of the bus honking.

MAXINE:

Well, this is just like last year.

JIMMY:
Am I takin' the bus?

MAXINE:
I think he deserves my truck.

JIMMY:
Or am I takin' Max's truck?

MAXINE:
I think he should.

JIMMY:
Mum?

MARLENE:
Dad?

MAXINE:
That's right Jim, step in.

MARLENE:
I'm not sayin' that, Mum.

JIMMY:
What are you sayin' for the second time!

MARLENE:
I'm askin' you, Dad.

MAXINE:
She's askin' you, Jim.

MARLENE:
I am not Mum.

JIMMY:
Do I or don't I?

MARLENE:
Well, take it or leave it—

JIMMY:
The bus or the truck?

MARLENE:

    See what I care—

JIMMY:

    The bus?

MARLENE:

    The truck.

MAXINE:

    How 'bout her car?

JIM:

    Maxine—

MAXINE:

    What!

JIM:

    (*to JIMMY*) Go wave, you won't ride today.

JIMMY:

    But I rolled my truck!

MARLENE:

    He's right, Dad.

MAXINE:

    Hey, we all end up in the ditch sooner or later.

JIM:

    Just go.

JIMMY:

    I had those beers!—I don't deserve the truck! I don't
want the truck, don't give me the truck!

JIM:

    Get!

        *JIMMY takes a step back. Everyone freezes. JIMMY tears
        out through the back door.*

MAXINE:

> Yeah ... so we get talkin' this West Edmonton Mall, huh, and I said to this couple, I said, "You know that shoppin' cenner don't hold a candle to Disneyland," and that Texan he was quick to agree.

> *She has taken the two cinnamon buns and put them on plates. She heads out, taking more menus. JIMMY comes racing back in.*

JIMMY:

> Okay, this is the kinda total jerk I am. I knew Dad was gonna marry Linda, I knew since July, I kep' it to myself. Day Mum gets clued into it I be this complete dolt to her, make her feel like sludge for not lettin' me take Max's truck.

> *Pause.*

JIM:

> Jimmy, it's understandable you didn't want to say anything to your mother.

JIMMY:

> No, it isn't, is it?

JIM:

> It is.

JIMMY:

> Eh?

JIM:

> Yes, Jimmy.

JIMMY:

> Oh.

MARLENE:

> It's—it's fine you didn't tell me, Jimmy. It's fine.

JIMMY:

> Thanks.

MARLENE:
Thanks?

JIMMY:
Fine.

MARLENE:
How old she, this gal?

Pause.

JIMMY:
Beg your pardon?

MARLENE:
Old.

JIMMY:
I don't really know, any girl over sixteen is old to me.

JIM:
Is she a responsible person, your mother means.

MARLENE:
If she's just some chick—

JIMMY:
Linda? She ... isn't much.

JIM:
Jimmy, sit down.

They all take a seat at the table. A long pause.

JIMMY:
Actually no, Linda's all right. I can't help it, she is. And she keeps him in line anyway—he even shows up on time for her and everything. We're headin' over to her place and Dad sees this tavern?—Automatically the guy just navigates into the parking lot. Looks over to me, shakes his head, says, "Second thought I don't really need that Budweiser—not if I know what's good for me"—slips it into reverse and we're outa there before we're even in. "Who is this girl got you so

71

turned around?" I says and he turns beet-red, my own
dad. I give him this cuff, eh, and he says, "You're
pretty damn cocky kid," and o' course he knows I
come by that naturally so that ended that. (*pause*) But
so, this Linda, she's really worked wonders—(*to JIM*)
Should I 'a said all this. I shouldn't've said all this,
should I have?

MARLENE:

No Jimmy, it's … fine. It's good your dad's like that to
her, it's … good.

JIMMY:

Well, I figgered it was.

MARLENE:

Then maybe you know about the house too?

JIMMY:

That, I didn't know.

MARLENE:

It's in a modern development, it's a big split-level,
bedrooms galore, full-size bathroom, prob'ly two even,
top o' the line furniture, colonial style he's decked
this gal out with.

JIM:

Marlene, do you know these details?

MARLENE:

No, I don't, but I can put two and two together as
good as anyone, even if I only got junior high.

JIMMY:

Did he say it was a split-level?

MARLENE:

It's nothin' shabby.

JIMMY:

Well, no, it wouldn't be, Linda goes in for quality, she had a great apartment, then see, she's been handling all their finances, Dad he signs his paycheques over to her and she put him on this allowance. 'Course with him not drinkin' so much he didn't spend so much and, well, Linda makes a darn good wage herself—

JIM:

Quiet, Jimmy.

JIMMY:

Pardon?

MARLENE:

Well what's this gal do, bank teller?

JIMMY:

She—I—it's slipped right from my mind.

MARLENE:

Slip it back.

Pause.

JIMMY:

She's ... nothin' but a second-rate secretary, prob'ly pours coffee all day, eh. (*JIMMY jumps up as he realizes what he has said. MARLENE goes to get the coffee pot, and her order pad, and exits to the front.*) I mean!—not that there's anything wrong with pourin' coffee—Grandad, I didn't mean—look at what we do, think starin' into the north end of a south bound cow's anything to write home about? Huh? Go tell her we're nothin' neither.

JIM:

You haven't had an honest breakfast today, have you?

JIMMY:

Breakfast? Yes ... no—I don't know.

JIM:

Well, sit down and put a decent meal in you.

JIMMY:

Sit down?—On what?—This gibbled chair, bent
cigarette pack underneath its leg? My thighs are so
tense they're gonna take off on their own—look,
they're puffin' in an' out—my dad's comin', the crop's
not off, you're losin' time like sixty bears and I'm
supposed to be a normal human Albertan and eat
breakfast?—Well, sorry Grandad, but Puff' Wheat is
just not gonna do it right now, not for this cowboy.

JIM:

It's a heckuva way for a guy to grow up, you're right.

JIMMY:

It's just total stress in here, all the time.

JIM:

I've noticed that too.

JIMMY:

Grandad, it's not funny, this is my life.

JIM:

I know that, Jimmy.

JIMMY:

American, Canadian—back, forth—like it mattered
what a guy was—why couldn't I've bin born in
Australia, nowhere near the American border?—I go
over to Nedchuk's place and he's got this complete
dream situation—furniture?—totally matches. Sit
down to eat and everybody's got their own place?—
little doo-dads on the window sill. His dad's got a
complete Black and Decker lifestyle down that
basement and his mum's all a'fluff her new living-
room curtains are a quarter-inch off. (*pause*) That
greaseball Nedchuk sits there beefin'a gripe about

how he can't blast his stereo. Me, I'm driving home in my truck and I'm thinkin' what I wouldn't give for a living-room window—never mind the quarter-inch-off curtains. (*pause*) Okay, I know, I can stay out the farm anytime I want but Max doesn't care about curtains, she's never even over there—Mum cares, but she's afraid to spend a dollar. She's "waitin'."

JIM:

Well, that's true.

JIMMY:

We should pour cement in this back suite, seal it off.

JIM:

Bulldoze the whole café.

JIMMY:

Nuke it right off the face of the earth. I'll tell you one thing, I'm not ever gettin' married—you can bet the rent on that. I'm gonna build a house. And it's gonna be bought and paid for before I put my wife into it. There's gonna be no make-do, half-done, wait-see about it.

JIM:

The girl you're not gettin' married to is sure gonna be set up right.

JIMMY:

And it's gonna have a reg'lar kitchen. With appliances rigged up from here to—to—to nowhere. Who am I tryna kid? (*The sound of a tanker going by.*) Let's face it, Grandad, there's … something seriously the matter with me.

JIM:

You figger?

JIMMY:

I swear to God if people knew the kindsa things find their way into this brain?—they'd have me committed. I cause myself embarrassment, it's no joke.

JIM:

Yeah, well, I'll admit I've had my suspicions about you.

JIMMY:

Eh?

JIM:

Sure. Time you were sittin' out in the middle o' the field there for'n hour'n a half. Now what's that kid up to? I thought. Out I go and your mouth was hangin' open and all the rest—you says, "Gonna be a fight tonight, Grandad." Well, the sun was goin' down on this side and the moon was comin' up on this side and you says to me, "A fight which one's prettier." Well, I knew then you didn't think too reg'lar.

JIMMY:

Yeah, but Grandad, it's gotten way worse than that.

JIM:

Worse you say.

JIMMY:

I start out okay but then before I know it I'm right off the tracks. Like when it's a house I'm gonna build, I get the spot all picked out and settle on a nice little bungalow. But it always happens I'm buildin' the house for Mum instead. And I'll be ridin' along in the combine, or ... drivin' my truck, and well, pretty soon that house has something real feasible like eighteen bathrooms—just this ignorant sprawl of a spread that people have to come from miles around just to gawk at. With binoculars. Holidays—I'd take Mum down to L.A. and deck her out with all these clothes—like Dad was always gonna—and she wouldn't have to serve nobody—we'd eat in fancy restaurants and—and Grandad, there's somethin' awful I gotta tell you.

JIM:

What Jimmy?

JIMMY:

I—I didn't have anything to drink the night I rolled my truck. I just said I had those three Canadians to gimme an excuse to do such a fried thing. I couldn't just roll it, not me, I had to smack into the telephone pole to boot. Look up and see fifty head o' cattle standin' there starin' at me like I'm dumber'n they are. I was buildin' the eighteen bathrooms when I rolled my truck, I was takin' Mum to classy restaurants—my mind was wandering, okay? All over the road. And so was the truck. That's the kinda bigshot I am. Bigshot like my old man. Can't even stay on the road.

JIM:

Well, Jimmy, I … don't know what to say.

JIMMY:

Please don't tell no one.

JIM:

That you'd bin grounded all summer 'cause you were stone cold sober?

JIMMY:

Uh, yeah. (*long pause*) Ya know Grandad, no offence. But you got a way about you that … just seems to narrow in on the idiot side of my personality. Only time I ever feel like I'm on the ball at all is when— well, is when I'm with my dad. I can bounce back and forth about goin' on those hauls but I know the minute I hear his rig pull up, I'll just all a' sudden wanna go. I forget everything when I get in that rig. Him and me, we cut-up somethin' terrible. I'm sorry

77

but he's just this hilarious guy, Grandad. And I'm pretty funny myself when I'm with him, figger that one out.

JIM:

There's nothing wrong with having a good time with your father.

JIMMY:

No? Then why do I gotta feel like sludge the minute I come back and see you? You, you're just this perfect human type-guy, never caused no one no trouble when you were a kid—ask anyone in this district, no one'll say a bad word about you—well try livin' up to that, Grandad.

JIM:

Oh, Jimmy, where you got such a silly notion of me—

JIMMY:

But no, I can't be your clone, I gotta have a father doesn't even know it's harvest—I can't just up and move with the crop not off. (*pause*) Can I?

JIM:

We're almost done. I can get Quint.

JIMMY:

Quint?

JIM:

Not gonna lie to you. You know I'm no fan of your father's. And it's not my belief that a boy should have to decide something like this in a day's time but that's Don.

JIMMY:

I'm not a boy, okay.

JIM:

Well, no, but I guess he figures it's better now than not at all.

JIMMY:

The fact that he wants me at all is pretty strange—I always thought the most my Dad could take o' me was four, five times a year, eh.

Pause.

JIM:

Maybe it'll be good for you to get away from all this haywire here. Enjoy yourself for awhile. The farm, well, it'll always be here.

JIMMY:

Geez, you sound like—aren't you—

JIM:

See Jimmy, when I was about your age—

MAXINE bursts through the door.

MAXINE:

I think that couple's Communist.

JIM puts his hat on and exits outside. JIMMY follows him as far as the door. MAXINE starts preparing orders.

MAXINE:

Me and that Texan got talkin' politics and how it's such a joke up here with three parties and how was I to know they'd belong to the third—well, her chin got that Thelma look and him, he started twitchin' his neck—they're prob'ly so left o' cenner they gotta hold onto the rails to keep from fallin' off. And to think they're headin' into America. Trust Russia to drop 'em down through Edmonton.

JIMMY has moved to his room.

JIMMY:

(*to himself*) Well Grandad's real tore up over all this, isn't he. Mum, she was down on her knees, beggin' me to stay. Guess I'll just have to pry myself away from them, break their hearts and move. Aw, there's no way, what am I talkin' about, it's just too late, the damage is done, I've already grown up. Canadian. Am I supposed to just pack up and move?—into that big ... split-level? Be a guy that hangs "a-out." Play their kinda football. I mean, there's no reason for me to—to go, there's just—there's ... gorgeous babes down there. American girls. And they're gonna be fallin' at my Canadian feet. Yeah right, Jimmy, you'll be a wipe-out down there just like you are up here. I could ... fake it though.

MAXINE has come towards JIMMY's room.

MAXINE:

Fake what?

JIMMY:

(*wheels around*) Whataya think of—of America, Max? (*pause*) I might move there, eh.

MAXINE:

Sure you might and you can take your Aunt Thelma and Her Majesty with ya—do 'em good to find out what real life is all about—instead o' sittin' up here with milk in their tea, makin' judgements.

JIMMY:

I might move there tonight, like.

MAXINE:

Huh?

JIMMY:

With my dad. Gonna have to say good-bye to this place, isn't that a shame?—Tell a guy—tell a guy why he'd wanna stay here when he can move into some swank place down the States. (*MAXINE is stunned. JIMMY looks at her.*) Say somethin', Max. Max.

MARLENE enters from the front.

MARLENE:

Two dailies, one ranchman no onions, two ones, one denver and a side o' browns. (*MARLENE looks to MAXINE. MAXINE looks back.*) Side … o' browns, Mum. (*pause*) Mum.

> *MAXINE moves to the junk drawer and fumbles for a Lucky. She lights it, having to keep her hand steady. She moves to the kitchen table and sits down. MARLENE looks to JIMMY. He takes the keys out of his pocket and goes out the back door, letting it flap shut. MARLENE goes to the coffee pot and pours MAXINE a cup. Music comes on the jukebox out front to end the act.*

ACT TWO

The front of the café. We are now on the other side of the order window and swinging door, and can see into the kitchen. There is a till booth area with rows of Lifesavers and chocolate bars. There is a phone by the cash register. Trophies, postcards and Canadian and American flags are about. Along the counter clusters of serviette canisters, salt and pepper shakers and sugar containers are evenly placed. Red leatherette stools are up to it. Behind it there is a milkshake-maker, pop machine, and coffeemaker, etc. There is a booth and a number of tables with a suggestion of the café existing beyond our view. We are looking through the wall and window of the café so that when the characters look toward us they are seeing the highway and prairie.

As another song comes to an end we can hear the sound of the combine fading in and out. The sun is starting to set, and will reach its peak at the close of the play.

A duffle bag, small suitcase, and hockey stick are placed together near the till. JIMMY, his hat on, is sitting sideways on a booth seat. Chocolate bar wrappers and potato chips are on the table. A tanker can be heard gearing up. JIMMY raises himself up slightly to listen. He slouches back down as the tanker gears by.

MAXINE enters from the kitchen. She is in jeans and a sweatshirt, and carrying Marlene's cigarettes. She places the pack on the counter, puts a coffee mug out, takes the coffee pot from the machine, and pours. She puts the pot back, staring heavily into it.

MAXINE:

Readin' this article, oh where was it. *Readers' Digest.* (*She heads around the counter to sit on a stool, keeping her back to JIMMY.*) Yeah, according to this article … nine outa ten Americans … carry guns. (*takes her lighter out and lights a cigarette*) Run across the line and get your Max a package o' Lucky's before I affixicate myself on these of your mother's—I'll handle it if your dad shows up while you're gone.

JIMMY:

(*not moving*) I bet you will.

MAXINE:

Believe it was in the state of Wyoming, speakin' of Wyoming, that this here nutcase done away with was it sixteen families?—on their way to church. He was prob'ly a Vietnam vet, 'course America had no business even goin' to Vietnam. Or to any of these other trouble spot countries, in my opinion. (*takes a drink of coffee*) Not to mention the moon. The moon, in my mind, should remain neutral. We got no business puttin' a claim on it. But violence in America is somethin' the Russians don't have. (*glances over her shoulder to see if JIMMY is paying attention*) Now you know I loved John Fitzgerald more than the brother I didn't have. The day that news come on the air from Dallas?—I was standin' in there makin' a grilled cheese sandwich. Yes. You think a Canadian would ever take a shot at their—I mean our prime minister? No. 'Course there were many that wrestled with the idea more'n they should've when Trudeau was in

83

power. (*takes a drag off her cigarette and butts it in disgust*)
Now you take television. The stuff they put on down
there? Trash. You wanna know the name of a good
program on TV and it's been on for twenty, thirty
years and it's Canadian, it's not American, it's on the
CBC and it's—the—the—it's bin on the years—it's—
oh, what the hell's the name o' that show? Well, you
know what one I mean, that one. Or how 'bout their
national sport, that's a sport?—spittin', chewin' and
scratchin' with the odd baseball tossed—and I don't
know why you're takin' all this hockey equipment.
Hockey isn't nothin' down there, it's not even played.

JIMMY:

They play hockey down there.

MAXINE:

Well, they shouldn't! They're gonna be beatin' yas at
your own game before much longer, and then sellin' it
back to you, that's the way these people operate, I was
raised down there, I know how they think—me, us,
we're first, we're best, gimme that—you wanna buy it?
(*pause*) Jimmy, America is just not the place you think
it is. It's not the place it used to be.

JIMMY:

Yeah, it seems to've changed an awful lot since this
morning even.

MAXINE:

What—what happens this girl sees the light like your
mother done and walks out on your dad. Then who's
gonna look after you?

JIMMY:

I don't need anyone to look after me. I can look after
myself, if you haven't noticed.

84

MAXINE:

> Everyone needs someone to look after 'em—or I mean, women don't, they got it built-in, but men, they do.

> > *JIMMY has gone to his gear and picked up his hockey stick.*

JIMMY:

> I don't. Any chick who gets serious with me is gonna have a few disappointments. (*fakes a slap shot*) 'Cause I'm not the kind to be held down, okay. (*puts the stick down*) Furthermore—

MAXINE:

> Oh good, I like these furthermores.

JIMMY:

> I'm takin' her out normal. To the show, to parties, dances—I'm givin' her everything she wants, we're gonna go out for a long, long time—years—and really get to know each other and then she's gettin' a proper ring, the whole bit—church, reception in the Elks Hall, and a two-week honeymoon. And it will be decades before any baby is born to wreck our happiness.

MAXINE:

> Jimmy.

JIMMY:

> I'm not rushin' into anything, got the picture?

MAXINE:

> I guess you're kinda like Grandad when it comes right down to it, huh?

JIMMY:

> You got it.

MAXINE:

Yeah, he knew me a day and a half before we got married.

JIMMY:

Well, fine, but that's another thing—I'm marrying someone same side o' the border.

MAXINE:

What side would this be?

The sound of a tanker. JIMMY looks out, seeing if it stops. It gears right on by.

JIMMY:

No side.

MARLENE enters. She is wearing jeans and a light sweater. Her appearance changes quite radically when not wearing her uniform. JIMMY wheels around at the sound of the tanker, and sees her enter.

JIMMY:

Super, Dad's now five hours late, Marlene.

MAXINE:

Is it after nine? (*to MARLENE*) You watchin' Dallas?

MARLENE:

You … go ahead and watch it, Mum.

MAXINE:

Huh?—oh. (*takes her coffee and heads toward the kitchen*)

JIMMY:

I only tell my coach I'm not gonna be around this year, I only tell all the guys, I only been holed up in this café since four lookin' out the window every— (*picks up his hockey stick and sets it back down*)—time a truck goes by.

86

MAXINE:

    (*at the door*) You go back to that school on Monday and tell everyone you changed your mind. They'll be so happy they'll throw a party for you.

JIMMY:

    Max, you seem to have this big idea that I'm someone at that school. I'm no one.

MAXINE:

    You're more'n your mother was.

JIMMY:

    Well, I maybe am but I'm not no hero.

MARLENE:

    I didn't have time for friends when I was rushin' back home to work dinner shift, but never mind, I—

MAXINE:

    You tell your coach you wanna try out for the team, he'll letcha, star player like you were last year. Huh, Mar?

JIMMY:

    Star.

MAXINE:

    You were the best player on the team last year, the league—ask your grandad.

JIMMY:

    Grandad?—All Grandad said was my coordination was improving. I didn't even know my coordination was bad.

MAXINE:

    It's not, it's excellent, it's cleared right up. I could catch a pop-fly when I was a kid, back home in Minnesota—I played with a soda jerk team, that's how good I was—you get your athaletic ability from my side.

MARLENE:

Mum, you don't have a side when it comes to Jimmy.

MAXINE:

Huh?

MARLENE:

He's got my side, and his dad's side.

MAXINE:

My side's your side.

MARLENE:

Your side's back home in Minnesota—and—and if you're gonna say I'm every inch Aunt Thelma—

MAXINE:

Oh, you never forget nothin' do you—

MARLENE:

—even though you wiped your American spit all over my face then don't try to inch me out of my own kid's half.

JIMMY looks to MARLENE, then abruptly away.

MAXINE:

Whataya pickin' on Maxine for?—I'm tryna talk the kid outa goin'. You don't see your dad in here, do ya?

MARLENE:

Dad's got a crop to get off.

MAXINE:

I know all about the crop, I bin playin' second fiddle to it since I come up here. And to you. Thelma, and her majesty mother-in-law over there with the tea-stained teeth. Ninety years old and not even a hint of poor health. Tellin' me I don't know how to put a meal on the table. Bin doin' it for a livin' all my life, which is somethin' neither of those two know sweet tweet about—living, or makin' one. Sittin' on their

88

royal haunches all their narrow lives—criticizin'. (*exits to the back*)

> MARLENE *and* JIMMY *exchange a look.*

MARLENE:
She's right, you know.

JIMMY:
That you take after them?

MARLENE:
No, that they're like that—do I take after them? I do, don't I—no, I don't.

JIMMY:
How should I know and who cares?

MARLENE:
Well, fine, but I'm not turnin' out like Thelma.

JIMMY:
You think Dad's had himself a wreck?

MARLENE:
No, I—I don't, Jimmy. Your dad's fine, he's just runnin' a little behind. He hasn't had himself a wreck.

JIMMY:
But what if he jack-knifed in his rush to get here?

MARLENE:
Well, that much I doubt for the very simple reason that your dad is a professional from the word go. And say it's a shifted load or somethin', well, that's gettin' fixed right this second, they service those big trucks reg'lar on that innerstate. And if it's not that, well, he coulda got away late.

JIMMY:
You said he'd be here at four.

MARLENE:

I shouldn't've said four, it's my fault. I shoulda just said I don't know. That's what—

JIMMY:

What?

MARLENE:

Well, that's what I used to do when you were a kid.

JIMMY:

You did?

MARLENE:

Sure. Or if he'd call when you were out I wouldn't tell you so you wouldn't wait, or if he didn't show up, well you'd be none the wiser. Then if he did, see, then you got a nice surprise. But I'd like to know why it is you think this is all you'll need down there, this tiny suitcase and that gear.

JIMMY:

(*looks to it*) Well, whataya think I should do? Just rip out the whole suite of every bit of evidence I ever lived here? Take all I own so I never have to show my face in here again?

MARLENE:

She's gonna think you don't have nothin'!—this is all I ever give ya. Take—take the ghetto blaster at least?— just take it and—oh, what am I sayin', they'll prolly have one, they'll have stereo equipment from here to—(*looking outside*)—that old gas pump.

> *MARLENE has gone to the window to look out. JIMMY stares out in the direction of the pump as well.*

JIMMY:

That pump should be bulldozed.

MARLENE:

The pump stays. And so does my ole Texaco star.

JIMMY:

Your ole Texaco star, that's my ole Texaco star.

MARLENE:

Used to tell folks, I'd say, you wanna find your way
back here, all you gotta do is look for the star.

JIMMY:

I never heard you say anything so stunned in your life
to anyone.

MARLENE:

When I was a kid. Life was goin' on a little bit before
you were born, you know. I was the kid around here at
one time.

JIMMY:

I can't help I was born.

MARLENE:

I used to watch those little coloured balls hop around
when the gas was pourin'—and if I had my way we'd
still have that pop machine out front, that Orange
Crush.

JIMMY:

It wasn't good for anything but slappin' shots against,
and you got no right to put a claim on the pump, or
the star. They aren't even ours. We never owned that
g'rage.

MARLENE:

You see anyone around here care a darn? You see
anyone wantin' to buy us out and put up a big
Voyajer? It's never gonna be a big draw in here.

JIMMY:

You wanna turn a profit, you gotta go one way or the
other. Which no one in this family can ever do.

MARLENE:

What're you talkin' about?

JIMMY:

Turn it back into a truck stop. Or upgrade into a restaurant. Who ever heard of a café on the bald-headed prairie with no place to gas up?

MARLENE:

We got those that remember us keepin' us afloat, we got a good clientele—and people make a point of stopping back—thanks to Mum.

JIMMY:

A place like this doesn't have a clientele, it's got reg'lars.

MARLENE:

That's right, Jimmy. But not everyone wants 'a go to a place 'its build around a salad bar they gotta feel guilty about. Get served parsley with a bran muffin by a waitress named Tom. Like the places up in Calgary. Nice way to bring up a kid. You coulda done worse. There's nothin' fancy about the Bordertown but you'll think more of it when you're gone. Think I liked it before I left? Gang from high school used to pile into their dads' Meteors and come in here for something to do. Well, I had to serve those boys. I was thirteen, fourteen years old. Jack Jaffrey would walk like me, talk like me, act the smart aleck in fronna all his friends? I'd say to Mum, I'm not goin' out there, I'm not no more—then I'd run out to the farm. (*This strikes her funny all of a sudden.*)

JIMMY:

Why you laughin'?—I'd like to beat the snot outa that guy.

MARLENE:

Well, never mind, poor Mum had to cook, serve, clear and do till all on her own—that's how rotten I was to her—I'd take off just like that, I'd go down the

coulees sometimes and Dad would have to get me.
Bring me back. That Jack Jaffrey ended up on drugs,
went the hippie route—grew his hair down to his rear-
end and hitch-hiked down to California.

JIMMY:

So, Dad, you don't think he's had a wreck?

MARLENE:

No, me, I was still poofin' my hair and wearin' stove
pipe pants when I got married.

JIMMY:

Yeah, well, fine.

MARLENE:

Fine what?

JIMMY:

Open up a museum in here. Keep the star, keep the
pump, plug a Canadian quarter into the jukebox and
an American quarter into Maxine and let her pour
forth with a few million stories about her fat cousins in
Oklahoma. Or how she come up here in '49. Nineteen
and dumber 'an a dawg.

MARLENE:

Oh crumb, you said it.

JIMMY:

Grandad and me are the only ones know it's the
present.

MARLENE:

Yeah? That farmhouse don't look too modern.

JIMMY:

There's nothin' wrong with that farmhouse, it's got a
good foundation.

MARLENE:

Got four kinds o' linoleum showin' through on the floor, should put indoor-outdoor down in there.

JIMMY:

Grandad's dad built that house, you don't rip that linoleum up, I like those other floors showin' through. I suppose I'll come back and you'll've talked Grandad into soakin' every last cent into somethin' him and me don't want.

MARLENE:

Whata you care? You're goin' to wall-to-wall plush carpet!

JIMMY:

Don't change nothin'!

MARLENE:

I won't! I won't get nothin' for myself, I won't get my bathroom—

JIMMY:

Never said nothin' 'bout in here!

MARLENE:

You want me to bulldoze the pump and star!

The sound of a tanker. They watch for it to gear down. It goes right on by.

JIMMY:

Great. Prob'ly chattin' up some chick.

MARLENE:

And another thing. Don't you—you—you get what I'm sayin'?

JIMMY:

Huh?

MARLENE:

> Don't you start bein' the—the smart aleck down there, like.
>
> > *Pause.*

JIMMY:

> I already am one. I'm a chip off the ole block.

MARLENE:

> You just—if the two of you? I mean it. Are somewhere and what have you. Okay? You think of that—you think of that Linda girl and you … (*taps her finger on the counter*) you make sure things stay right for her.

JIMMY:

> How?

MARLENE:

> Well.

JIMMY:

> Huh?

MARLENE:

> No, but I'm sayin' you just be responsible when you meet a girl, and what-all.

JIMMY:

> Meetin' 'ems one thing, gettin' 'em to go out with you's another.

MARLENE:

> Jimmy?

JIMMY:

> What?

MARLENE:

> Don't be … in a hurry.
>
> > *Pause.*

JIMMY:

> (*moving away*) Where is he, Mum?

MARLENE:

> Get your grade twelve and you do … good and do …
> good.

> *JIMMY is looking outside. MARLENE starts to go to him,
> to touch him, but he turns around and she moves away.*

JIMMY:

> Why isn't Grandad comin' in off the field to say good-
> bye?

MARLENE:

> He said so at supper and he's—he's stayin' out there.

JIMMY:

> He didn't say nothin', I was doin' till—he stayed in
> there. (*toward the kitchen*) He figures I should be out
> there workin' 'steada sittin' on my lazy butt in here.

MARLENE:

> You had to go to school, you had to tell people, the
> bank.

JIMMY:

> So I'm here since four afraid to bring the cows in or
> do my milkin' 'case Dad shows up, sees I'm not
> chompin' at the bit to hop on up. Grandad has to ask
> Quint. Quint. Pickin' up my slack.

MARLENE:

> You know what I'm gonna miss? I'm gonna miss, uh,
> seein' the hockey games, and what-all.

JIMMY:

> You're kidding?

MARLENE:

> That hat trick you scored, type-thing, eh. (*pause*) Last
> year.

JIMMY:

> Well what about it?

MARLENE:

I'm just sayin'.

JIMMY:

Yeah, that was quite the fluke, that night.

MARLENE:

Really? Oh. Well, did you want something to eat?

JIMMY:

Eat?

MARLENE:

Eat.

JIMMY:

Like what?

MARLENE:

Well, food or somethin', whatja have for supper?

JIMMY:

Hot beef san'wich.

MARLENE:

This gal cook?

JIMMY:

Whata you all a' sudden care if I get a balanced diet or not?

MARLENE:

You eat reg'lar.

JIMMY:

Yeah, I eat with 'em too, I'm just reg'lar around here, like Wally and Quint—that's how I eat reg'lar.

MARLENE:

Well, what do you want?

JIMMY:

A salad bar.

MAXINE enters, drinking a Coke.

MAXINE:

> I seen that one.

MARLENE:

> Mum, Jimmy wants a salad bar in here.

MAXINE:

> Why didn'tcha say?—We'll haul that jukebox out and set 'er up there.

MARLENE:

> I don't want that jukebox hauled out.

MAXINE:

> Let's knock out a wall.

JIMMY:

> I don't want a wall knocked out.

MARLENE:

> He's sayin' I don't feed him reg'lar meals.

MAXINE:

> We get goin' on this it could be done by Monday.

JIMMY:

> My dad's had a wreck, she's knockin' out walls.

MARLENE:

> He hasn't had a wreck and look in that fridge.

JIMMY:

> Well, it would be just my loser-luck if he did have a wreck.

MARLENE:

> There's a tub o' coleslaw in there day in and day out.

JIMMY:

> Okay, never mind the coleslaw, never mind the walls.

MAXINE:

> Your grandad and me nearly had a divorce over that wallpaper—see that buckin' bronc there with the twisted leg?—I took Marlene's brown crayon and coloured

that in—when Jim come in from coolin' off over me handin' him the one strip upside down, he took one look at my artwork and—see this roof? (*points up*) He hit it. He was always horrible to live with, even then.

MARLENE:

(*leaving to the back*) He doesn't care about the roof, the wallpaper—thirty years old and still holdin'—he doesn't care about anything—I didn't feed him reg'lar meals.

JIMMY:

(*watches her leave and goes after her*) I do so care!

MAXINE:

(*looks to the back, then to JIMMY*) Yeah!

JIMMY:

Yeah, what Max?

MAXINE:

What about the time you fired the hardball through the window there?

JIMMY:

If I was gonna be five hours late I'd call a guy and she's the one that don't care.

MAXINE:

Your mother was ready to sell you to the Hutterites for a nickel that day. I'm the one stuck you under the counter 'til she seen the humour. It was me that risked an early death every Christmas climbin' onto the roof to put Sanny Claus up there with his nose blinkin' off and on in thirty below weather. It was me that shovelled the ditch so the kid could play hockey when he come home from school, not his Canadian grandad out in that field.

JIMMY:

Grandad said goodbye at supper.

MAXINE:

> (*grabbing him*) Tell your Max you're not goin' down there, tell her you wanna stay home. (*hugs him*)

JIMMY:

> (*moving away*) Yeah well, "home."

MAXINE:

> What about—

JIMMY:

> (*wheeling around*) What about that Cuisanart I boughtcha?—Eh? Think that come cheap? I sprung two hunderd Canadian for that rig and you haven't even touched it. It sits over at the farm collectin' dust.

MAXINE:

> I don't do enough cookin' here I gotta cook there?

JIMMY:

> And come winter, I wancha to start spendin' more time in that curling rink. Grandad likes that.

MAXINE:

> I am not sittin' … in no curlin' rink with a bunch o' whiny wives drinkin' coffee outa a styrofoam cup.

JIMMY:

> Oh sure, yet you sit in the hockey rink other side the buildin' watchin' me play.

MAXINE:

> He wants someone to watch him he's got Marlene.

JIMMY:

> She liked my hat trick.

MAXINE:

> She wasn't even there—oh yeah, that's right, she was. (*pause*) Oh boy, that was somethin', that hat trick.

JIMMY:

> Eh?

MAXINE:

You deserved your steak dinner that night, I'll tell ya.

JIMMY:

(*picks up his stick and does a shot in slow motion*) You know, I can't even think about that night without feelin' goosebumps. It's almost like it wasn't supposed to happen. I mean, lotsa guys score hat tricks. But, oh, if you woulda known how much I wanted to have a three goal game, all my life, just please God, let me score a hat trick. Me, I'm the kinda guy gets the odd goal if the other team's lousy. Or if their goalie's got the flu. My mind wanders. I think about my skating, I forget I got a stick. But that night, we were even playin' against an okay team. And it was one, two, three in the net before I knew what was happening.

MAXINE:

You musta had horseshoes up your patooie that night! Huh?

A tanker goes by. JIMMY looks to it.

JIMMY:

Yeah. That's all it was. Luck. A fluke.

MAXINE:

Huh?

JIMMY:

But my dad wouldna known luck from skill, he's never even been to a hockey game. He woulda thought I was great. Had he been there. (*pause*) Max?

MAXINE:

Yeah?

JIMMY:

I thought he was. He said he was gonna, and I kep' lookin' over by the entrance there thinkin' this man was him, same jacket, eh. You can't see worth a darn on that ice.

MAXINE:

You mean that's why you played so good?

JIMMY:

But it's these darn dispatchers, eh. They hold a trucker up somethin' terrible.

MAXINE:

Yeah. I heard that one before.

JIMMY:

It's true.

MAXINE:

No, I know, you're right.

JIMMY:

He tried, he tried real hard to make that game, I know for a fact he did. Linda even said when I was down in July, she told me lotsa stuff. When she first met him, he took out his wallet and showed her my picture. He didn't pretend like he didn't have a son. Like he coulda done. Only thing is the picture was from grade five or somethin', but so—it's a shifted load is all it is right now, and they're servicin' it right this—this minute.

MAXINE:

That's probably it.

JIMMY:

No, it isn't. (*pause*) Don't take five hours to fix a load. If he's—Max, if—he hasn't even bin married to her a month.

MAXINE:

Oh, Jimmy, your dad's—

JIMMY:

What Max?—what's my dad?—a saint? Huh? No. Well,
I clicked in to that a long time ago, okay. First time he
took me down to Texas it kinda sunk in. Boy oh boy,
he was takin' me to the lonestar state, I was gonna
have somethin' to brag about to the guys when I come
back. Mum had me workin' till all summer to save up
for those Cooperalls but Dad shows up end o'
August—well, somehow his sweet talk to the ladies
down there started seemin' a little more'n friendly,
put it that way. And the more he talks the more it hits
me—math's not my favourite subject but I'm addin'
up the years I'm alive with the years he's bin "seeing"
this one and that one and it's equalling the same
thing—he was two-timin' on Mum before I was even
born. After. And probably during. Well, I just couldn't
wait to get back here, take out my savings and—
(*pause*) Somehow those dumb little diamond earrings
Mum wanted were more important that a pair of
Cooperalls. You figger that out. (*MARLENE comes in from
the back, but JIMMY cannot see her.*) All day dumb junk
like that keeps comin' to me—like my whole life just
decides to show up in my head, in Panavision. And
still—still Max, I can't help thinkin' how hard Dad's
tryin' now and he's got Linda—she's just a way better
wife for him than Mum ever was—she's really neat, so
easy to talk to eh, like I can say whatever I want to her,
she's a little like you—when she's got somethin' to say?
she just says it—

MAXINE:

(*noticing MARLENE*) Oh geez Jimmy—

JIMMY:

No Max, lemme tell you—Linda's got a real way about
her. (*MARLENE exits.*) I don't know how Dad managed
to get her. Or Mum, for that matter. Women are just

like that, they're stupid when it comes to men. But
Max, can you see what I mean?—my dad's finally givin'
me somethin' I want. Not some bike or toy that I—I
used to leave out in the parkin' lot for some
Oldsmobile to back up over. Grandad can say I got no
value for the dollar—yeah, Grandad, that's why I saved
every penny I ever earned just so I could blow it on—
(*pause*) My dad's bin promisin' me this all my life.
Okay, it's a little late. And Mum's not gonna be a part
of it. But I quit dreamin' that one a long time ago.
And I know I gotta leave the guys, hockey, the farm,
Grandad and Mum but—

MAXINE:

What about your Max, gonna miss her?

MARLENE:

(*re-entering before JIMMY can answer*) I'll see ya then
Jimmy, I'm goin' out to the farm, eh.

JIMMY:

Pardon?

MAXINE:

The farm?

MARLENE:

Yeah, so—

JIMMY:

What for?

MARLENE:

Whataya think, my bath. (*a tanker goes by*) There he is.

JIMMY:

(*wheels around, willing it to be his dad*) That's not him,
Marlene. Did ya hear the rig gear down? No. Is there
an engine purrin' out there? No. 'Cause he's not here,
he might never get here and you'll be stuck with me.
He mighta changed his mind—he don't phone me,

I'm just supposed to know. He maybe decided he doesn't want the kid after all—I miss school, miss hockey, miss everything so I can wait. Wait for him like you used to, like you wait for some wonderful thing to happen with your life—some fairy tale ending—yeah, the unicorn collection is all she thinks about, well, isn't that right on the money, she's never gonna get outa here, she just stays in this café mornin', noon and night.

MAXINE:

Jimmy, your mom goes out.

JIMMY:

She doesn't go "a-out." You can't even get her to go to a dance.

MAXINE:

She'll come around.

JIMMY:

When? The woman's only been divorced since I was twelve.

MAXINE:

Yeah, well, when you were twelve you weren't too keen on your mother even talkin' to a man in here, never mind goin' out with one.

MARLENE:

Thank-you, Mum.

> MARLENE goes to the till area. JIMMY heads to the door, but wheels around.

JIMMY:

How could I say that to her? How? I can't believe I got so little goin' for me I actually say that-all to her the day I'm leavin'—I don't deserve no father, I don't deserve a home, that's why Dad's not showin' up, he's

105

thinkin' twice about havin' a smart-mouth like me
screw up his life again.

MAXINE:

Again—you listen here kid, you didn't screw up his
life. He screwed up ours, the day she run off with him.

MARLENE:

"She" didn't run off with no one. You're the one
figgered the sun rose and set on Don, he was an
American—he was gonna just "have to drop on back
next time he was up this way."

MAXINE:

I say that to everyone! And I can't help it if you were
too shy to talk to him yourself.

MARLENE:

Mum, I was fifteen.

MAXINE:

You were the oldest fifteen-year-old I ever come across.
I didn't know what to do with her from the time she
was this high. (*pause*) Yes, I liked Don. No, I don't see
through people. And I didn't listen to Jim. Like I
shoulda. But I seen my girl's eyes light up for the first
time the day Don walked in this café. (*looks to JIMMY*)
And now he's comin' to take you across that border
and all you tell your Max is how she liked your hat
trick. (*JIMMY looks abruptly away from MARLENE.*) How
you'll miss Grandad. Am I always gonna be alone in
this family?

JIMMY:

Alone?

> *The sound of the back door.*

MARLENE:

Here Dad is now, so you just quit talkin' nuts, Mum, I
mean it.

MAXINE:

Not talkin' nuts, all this kid thinks to say to me is go sit in the curlin' rink, pay attention to Grandad. Does Grandad ever pay attention to me?

JIM walks in, stopping at the door. He is exhausted and dusty.

MAXINE:

Huh?

JIM:

What's goin' on?

MAXINE:

Brings me up here after a day and a half and puts me in that farmhouse with his ditzy mother, gotta change her dress to say hello. Well, my folks didn't have sit-down meals. I not only had to raise myself, I had to raise my mom in the bargain. 'Cause my mother was useless. And my dad was no screamin' hell either—when he was there. So don't expect me to walk in that farmhouse and balance a china teacup on my knee, too nervous to know what to do but talk. They all in that family were just too good for me, you none o' ya involve me like I count, never have.

JIM:

What she on about this for?

MAXINE:

"She"—"leave her"—like I'm some kinda spoiled brat you have to put up with. Husband don't talk to me, doesn't think I'm bright enough. Maxine, she's just a dumb American. S'what you-all think deep down, I know you do.

JIM:

Jimmy, what in the hell is goin' on in here?

JIMMY:

I hurt Max's feelings real bad, it's all my fault.

MAXINE:

Kid's leavin', Jim. Care? I'm the only one showin' I do only to find out I'm the only one he's not gonna have a hard time leavin'.

JIMMY:

Max, that's not true.

MAXINE:

(*to JIM*) You, you're just so afraid all the time o' what I'm gonna do or say if I'm let in on anything. Ever stop to think while you're out in that field that I bin here pushin' forty years and I haven't done nothin' yet?

JIMMY:

Max, you done plenny, you're my Max.

MARLENE:

Shush, Jimmy.

JIMMY:

You shush.

JIM:

Memory serves me correct, day I brung you up here you turned around and went right back.

MARLENE looks to JIMMY. JIMMY looks to JIM.

JIMMY:

No way.

JIM:

Yes, she did. I think walkin' out on me is how you'd put it. Because that's what she did—straight through that field there. Across the border. She had no trouble leaving me.

Pause.

MAXINE:

I wouldn't say that. I run my nylon on the barb-wire.

JIM:

That's right, you did. I was married to her three days,
I'd known her five.

MAXINE:

Two of which were spent on the train waiting for
Saskatchewan to end.

JIM:

We got picked up at the station in Lethbridge and—

MAXINE:

His dad didn't say one word to us the whole time
home. Side by side in that old truck. Me in the
middle, a carbon copy on either side, lookin' straight
ahead. Walk into that farmhouse expectin' I don't
know what and what does the woman do but warm the
teapot. Hands me her best English china just hopin'
I'd break it, which I did.

JIM:

It wasn't her best, it was just some cup I got at the
show.

MAXINE:

Yeah, but I didn't know that.

JIM:

You didn't have to take off.

JIMMY:

I can't believe this on the day I'm leavin'.

MAXINE:

You didn't have to come after me.

JIM:

Well, I did.

    Pause.

MAXINE:

That's right you did and I'd like to know what for—
you-all get along just fine without me.

JIM:

I don't know about that.

MAXINE:

Huh.

JIM:

Said I don't know whereas we would, in fact, get along
without you. Maxine.

Pause.

JIMMY:

Told ya Max, the man needs ya—it's emotional
security.

JIM slowly looks at JIMMY.

JIM:

(*to MAXINE*) Speaking of tea.

MAXINE heads to the kitchen to prepare it. Pause.

JIM:

Much of a dinner crowd?

MARLENE:

Yes.

JIMMY:

No. Yes, I mean.

*JIM walks over to the gear and case and stares at it. He
goes to the window and takes a look out. He takes a
deep breath. He takes his hat off and wipes his brow.*

JIMMY:

I know I shoulda bin out there! I know I didn't even
do my chores! You don't have to stand there not tellin'
me!

JIM:

Well, I didn't expect you to today.

JIMMY:

No sooner would I leave he'd show up and how'd he take that? Huh?

MARLENE:

Jimmy, don't snap at Grandad, he's gonna wish he never come in.

JIMMY:

You snap at Maxine lef', right, and cenner, look how you talk to your own mother, Marlene.

JIM:

Here you kids.

MARLENE:

My mother is my mother.

JIMMY:

Oh, good one, Mum, and who're you?—Way you talk to Max is just pathetic.

JIM:

Jimmy, listen to yourself son.

JIMMY:

Son?—I'm not your son. I never will be, okay? So quit tyin' my stomach up in knots when he's not here yet and I shoulda bin out in that field all along. (*pause*) Good one, Jimmy. Insult Grandad now.

JIM:

Never mind.

MARLENE:

We're none of us what we're supposed to be in this family. Mum's like my daughter half the time, Jimmy's more of a brother. Guess it's no wonder he's itchin' to go south, eh Dad? He's got a new and improved father and a perky little secretary real eager to take my place.

Gee, you know Dad, this gal?—she's got a real way about her.

JIMMY:

You heard me.

MARLENE:

Jimmy can say whatever he wants to her, isn't that great? Wonder if he'll lip her off like he does me. 'Course I'm no one. I pour coffee all day. Raised in the back suite of the Bordertown Café like I had no choice but to tie on an apron, work till, cash out and close up. Time I was fifteen I could run this place. So what? Is that what I wanted? Who cares what I want— he can show me up all he wants to his dad and her, packin' this piddly little amount like it's all I could afford.

JIM:

Marlene.

MARLENE:

Well, Dad, I give him more'n a hockey stick to show them off.

JIMMY:

I don't want her to show them off, I don't want nothin' from her, Grandad.

MARLENE:

Yes, you do. You want something I just don't have. And never will. When I got somethin' to say, I can't just say it to you. I'm not her, I'm not the kinda wife your dad needed. I'm not my mother, I'm not Aunt Thelma, I'm no one—just myself. I got a few dollars in the Bank o' Montreal, I got a car, I'm thirty-four years old with fallen arches and sore back. But you know what? I like this place. And any changes I make I wanna make in my own good time. But first, I'm gonna … tra-vel.

Pause.

JIMMY:

Travel?

JIM:

Travel—?

MARLENE:

Booked my flight today. To Hawaii. And I'm goin'.
Come Christmas. Two weeks accommodation. Wardair.
You said I needed a holiday. Well, I'm takin' one.

JIMMY:

Whataya mean you're goin' to Hawaii? By yourself?

MARLENE:

Well, this is it.

> *MAXINE enters with a small pot of tea. She sets it on the counter.*

JIMMY:

Max, Mum's goin' to Hawaii!

MAXINE:

Huh!—How?

MARLENE:

Gonna dog-paddle, Mum.

MAXINE:

Hawaii?—Hawaii's part o' the United States.

JIMMY:

I'm not spendin' Christmas with my dad and her. I
don't even know them for nothin'. Aren'tcha even
gonna invite me home?

MAXINE:

I'll get Sanny Claus up and bakes my turkey and we'll
have all the reg'lars in—it'll be just the same without
her.

113

JIMMY:

You mean we aren't gonna be together ever again?
You mean this is it? The guy calls and I'm booted out
the door?

MARLENE:

Max'll give you a Christmas.

A tanker goes by. JIMMY ignores it.

JIMMY:

Mum, listen to reason, you can't go off single like that.
There's jerks out there. And—and you're easy prey,
especially when you get dressed up.

MARLENE:

I won't get dressed up. I'll wear my uniform over there
and carry a coffee pot.

MAXINE:

Thought you said your mother could do with a good
time for a change?

JIMMY:

Oh, yeah, but don't you think someone should go with
her?

JIM:

Jimmy should go with you, Marlene. He's right.

JIMMY:

No!—I didn't mean me.

MARLENE:

Well, he could if he … wants.

Pause.

JIMMY:

Want me to?

MARLENE:

(*looks to him, then away*) She'll prob'ly have somethin'
planned for you down there, a real Christmas, nice

homey stuff, fix that place up like you wouldn't
believe—your dad'll have so many presents for you
under that tree—

JIMMY:

Yeah, he's prob'ly planning it all right now, which is
why he's so late—but fine, I won't go with you, who
cares? I only bin waitin' in this café for the man since I
was four—I mean, I mean since four—but I'll keep
waitin', because it's what you want, I'll just—just—
(*takes out his wallet and fumbles for a piece of paper*)—give
you this now and take my gear and go stand out on
the highway, I'll just get outa your sight, Mum—
(*throwing the paper at her*)—so here, have it, okay?—It's
your pink bathroom. It's all paid for, it's looked after,
it's what you wanted, it's what you got—white bathtub,
pink curtains, flower wallpaper, just like the
magazines. You tell the man when he comes Monday,
clean, new, modern—exactly how you got it in your
head.

    Pause.

MAXINE:

Kid bought a bathroom. When what she got is fine.

MARLENE:

No, it's not fine. A person can hardly turn around in
there. There's no place to put my make-up on.

MAXINE:

Oh. You're right. The whole suite should be gutted.

MARLENE:

No, it shouldn't, just the bathroom.

MAXINE:

Just the ... bathroom.

MARLENE:

I didn't wanna buy the Mathison house, I wanted to stay here. I—I try to teach the kid the value of the dollar, I make him work till, I look in the window at those diamond chip earrings, I—and now he's put the mon—the money down on a bathroom.

Pause.

JIMMY:

I didn't even know you wanted Hawaii though. I figgered it was just the bathroom you wanted, eh.

MARLENE breaks down completely. JIMMY looks to JIM, to MAXINE, back to MARLENE.

JIMMY:

I can't believe I didn't think of Hawaii.

MAXINE gets a serviette from the canister and hands it to JIMMY. JIMMY goes to MARLENE to give it to her. She reaches out to get it but grabs onto JIMMY's hand instead. She keeps a distance from him, but brings his hand to her face and holds it there.

JIMMY:

You never even mentioned Hawaii.

MARLENE comes away and rushes to the back suite.

JIM:

Go after her, Maxine.

MAXINE exits.

JIMMY:

Trust me to come up with a bathroom.

JIM:

Sit down, Jimmy.

JIMMY sits on one of the stools up to the counter. JIM goes around the counter and reaches under it to a hiding spot. He pulls out a bottle of Canadian Club whiskey.

JIMMY is floored. He watches as JIM takes two glasses and pours two shots.

JIMMY:

Grandad. Are you really doing this?

JIM hands JIMMY a drink. JIMMY takes it.

JIM:

I'm a degenerate, there's no gettin' around it.

JIM comes around the counter and sits beside JIMMY. He clinks his glass with JIMMY's. They drink.

JIMMY:

Grandad?

JIM:

Yep.

JIMMY:

Just tell me if I'm doin' the right thing, goin' down there. That's all I wanna know.

JIM:

Can't tell you that.

JIMMY:

Maxine tells me.

JIM:

Do you listen? No. You still pack your kit.

JIMMY:

You don't like my dad though. That's sayin' something.

JIM:

He's not all bad.

JIMMY:

You don't like him, just say you don't like him.

JIM:

Not for me to say.

JIMMY:

Okay, now what don't you like about him?—that he doesn't show up on time, fine. He's not reliable. Now you see where I get it from.

Pause.

JIM:

Expecting an answer to that?

JIMMY:

Yeah.

JIM:

It's a load o' horseshit. (*takes a drink*) Blood only goes so far. It depends what a person sees around him. Some people, like your dad, they for whatever reason think they need the nonsense in life. That's not your problem.

JIMMY:

But Linda, she won't stand for it.

JIM:

So you tell me. However, who's to say how long her dent will last. Other hand, to be fair, maybe your dad is ready to quit playin' the man, and start bein' one. Before his son beats him to it. (*pause*) Which by God I think you already have.

JIMMY gets up to hide his reaction. He goes to the window to look out across the prairie. The sun is very low now and the light in the café is turning gold and pink.

JIM:

You … do a good day's work, Jimmy. I—well, I want you to know I'm proud of you.

JIMMY:

(*closes his eyes*) Yeah? (*pause*) How come I lip off my mum so bad?

Pause.

JIM:

You get that from your grandmother. Don't worry about your mum. She's had the misfortune of taking after me. So give her time.

JIMMY:

I'm runnin' outa time.

JIM:

Jimmy, get yourself in the driver's seat. You're lettin' your dad take the reins, take control of your life, waitin' on him like this. You want somethin' outa this bargain, but don't you think he does too? Eh? If he calls, you give him a time and if he doesn't meet it, well, that's his loss. He'll meet it.

JIMMY:

He won't meet it, that's just it.

JIM:

Prepare yourself for that. But Jimmy, don't chase after somethin' unless it's worth having.

JIMMY:

That why you chased after Max? You knew?

A long pause.

JIM:

I didn't know. I was just turned twenty.

JIMMY:

You didn't know?—And yet you went and married her?

JIM:

Okay.

JIMMY:

And then you went after her over that border when she caught her nylon? It just doesn't sound like you,

Grandad. I never stopped to think of it before, but marryin' Max so fast and chasin' her across the field, I just thought, boy, Grandad?

JIM:

I wasn't called Grandad in those days. (*pause*) I was called Jimmy.

JIMMY:

Your whole family prob'ly starin' at you out the window.

> *JIM sits down. JIMMY sits down beside him. They both look out.*

JIM:

It was rainin'.

JIMMY:

You get all muddy?

JIM:

My dad was ready to carve my ass for supper.

JIMMY:

Why?

JIM:

Well, I hadn't phoned home from Minnesota to say I was bringin' home a wife. He, of course, didn't even approve of me goin' in the first place.

JIMMY:

Down the States?

JIM:

Actually they thought I was in Manitoba.

JIMMY:

What?

JIM:

And we were right in the middle of seeding.

JIMMY:

You lef' him stranded? You left him—

JIM:

I wasn't all that keen on work back then.

JIMMY:

Huh?

JIM:

Chap I met in the Army, from Winnipeg, he had his eye on this Minnesota girl, see. Made the mistake of showin' me her picture. I got it in my head I'd go to Winnipeg, get him to take me down there, introduce us, eh.

JIMMY:

You didn't go down for an auction?

JIM:

Well, no, that was just the line.

JIMMY:

But Grandad—Max still thinks it was just chance, an auction you happened to go down for—didn't you tell her—after you were married and stuff?

Pause.

JIM:

Well, I've been meaning to. But it's not the sort of thing a person likes to admit to. Especially knowin' it'd be general knowledge to anyone who happened to drop in here for coffee. Goin' all the way to Minnesota on the basis of a two-inch photograph your buddy happens to show you in Halifax?

JIMMY:

Halifax? You were in Halifax?

JIM:

I was there when the war ended.

JIMMY:

Wait a sec', wait a sec'—you mean to say—this is just hittin' me—you bin off the prairies?

Pause.

JIM:

Drink up, Kid. (*They drink.*) The prairies may be dry, but it was a different kind o' dry in Halifax, when the war ended. We could've done with a little of this then. We couldn't get a bottle o' beer, never mind this.

JIMMY:

Why not?

JIM:

Banned.

JIMMY:

You mean you couldn't celebrate?—What'd you do?

JIM:

Well. Not that I was instrumental, but we—we rioted.

JIMMY:

You rioted?

JIM:

Until they threw me in the clinker.

The phone rings. JIMMY jumps.

JIMMY:

My dad! (*The phone rings again. JIMMY looks to the back suite.*) I'm gettin' it in here! (*He goes to the phone and stares at it.*)

JIM:

Answer it.

JIMMY:

(*to himself*) Grandad rioted.

JIM:

Pick up the phone.

JIMMY:

>(*picking up*) Bordertown Café. Hi Dad.

>>*MAXINE and MARLENE enter.*

MARLENE:

>Where's he at?

JIMMY:

>(*into phone*) Where you at, Dad? (*cupping the phone*) Hasn't left. Yeah? Oh, is that it, eh?—uh huh. Yeah, well, that happens. Tie you up all day like that. (*cupping the phone*) Truck's just gettin' loaded now.

>>*MARLENE moves to the booth to sit down. MAXINE stays behind the counter. JIM sits as he was. They all stare out, as the sun continues to change.*

JIMMY:

>So I guess you … never thought to give us a call? No I know you're callin' now but it's late now—well, never mind, it—it doesn't matter. Eh? Yeah, well this is what Mum was sayin' you said. Pardon? Yeah, I know Linda likes me, why shouldn't she like me, I'm a good guy, eh. Chip off the ole block, right? Eh? Boy, that sounds pretty snazzy Dad. Twelve hunderd square feet, eh. How many? Boy. Two bathrooms? Wow, that's a lot. Uh huh. Yeah, well, I'd like to come down, sure—how big's the living-room? Is that right? Is that right? (*cups the phone*) Gotta buy more furniture to fill it up. Family room off the kitchen. (*goes back to the phone*) Dad, it sounds just great, I can hardly wait to see it, I'm all packed and—and what was the reason you said you didn't call? Call, Dad, call. Whataya mean why?—because I bin waitin', I had to—to miss hockey, I couldn't do chores for fear of missin' you, and it turns out you weren't even gonna phone to let a guy know? When I got a crop to get off? That wasn't fair, Dad, it just wasn't and I'm thinkin' maybe I'll take a pass on

movin' down there actually. But, uh, uh how be it I
come see you at Christmas? Oh heck, hold on,
Christmas is no good, I've already told Mum I'd take
her to Hawaii. Yeah, well, I checked around and found
a deal with Wardair, figgered she'd like to see the
place—you know how it is, we're not caught up in
spending a lot o' money on houses, we'd rather …
travel. Grandad was just tellin' me about Halifax, it's
got quite the history, he was there not too long ago—
anyhooo—(*cups the phone*) Can you believe what I'm
sayin'? (*goes back to the phone*) Tell you what I'm gonna
do for ya, Dad. Why don't you just think about
droppin' in on me next haul so I can know when to be
in the café. Like you sayin' next Friday, well, Friday's a
twenty-four hour day and I can't sit around here
waitin' for you to show up. Guess my point is in a few
weeks I'll be eighteen and—and what it boils down to
is you're eighteen years too late, Dad. I gotta be up at
four-thirty tomorrow, so I'll say good night, you keep
in touch, bye. (*He hangs up abruptly. He stares at the
phone. He looks up.*) That's not what I was gonna say.

MAXINE:
We shoulda put booze in that kid's bottle when he was
a baby and saved ourselves a lot o' trouble.

MARLENE:
It wasn't the liquor, Mum.

JIMMY:
Now I'll never see my dad.

JIM:
I suspect you'll see more of him.

JIMMY:
Mum, I blew it.

MARLENE:
Put your stuff in the back suite.

JIMMY:

Maybe I should phone back and apologize.

MARLENE:

And maybe you shouldn't. (*She holds a look with him. Then she goes to pick up some of his gear.*)

JIM:

Listen to your mother. (*JIMMY heads to his things. He picks up the remainder. He looks to JIM.*) I'll finish up tonight, you start in the morning.

> *MARLENE exits to the back. JIMMY follows her, looking back to him.*

JIMMY:

That is definitely not what I was gonna say. (*exits*)

> *JIM looks out at the sun setting.*

MAXINE:

Jim.

JIM:

What.

MAXINE:

Did you hear that kid talk to his dad?

JIM:

Yep.

MAXINE:

That's the American finally comin' out in him. (*JIM looks to her.*) Huh?—Good ole American gumption.

JIM:

(*puts on his hat*) Yeah, I guess that's what it is all right.

> *Pause.*

MAXINE:

Well, are you just gonna sit there?

JIM:

No. (*gets up and heads to the door*) Gonna get back out to the field.

He goes out, letting the screen door flap behind him. MAXINE looks after him, then goes out through the kitchen.

END